AMANDA LENOX
Biography

Healing Toward Wholeness

TABLE OF CONTENTS

CHAPTER 1
Claustrophobia

CHAPTER 2
Possessed

CHAPTER 3
Ikigai

CHAPTER 4
Tutto Fa Brodo

CHAPTER 5
Desire

CHAPTER 6
Amicus Fidelis Protectio Fortis

CHAPTER 7
Tunnels

CHAPTER 8
Tapestries

CHAPTER 9
Just Enough and Not at All

CHAPTER 10
Self-Help

CHAPTER 11
Public Property

CHAPTER 12
Defensive Maneuvers

CHAPTER 13
Just Ignore It

CHAPTER 14
The Bunker

CHPATER 15
Ex-Conned

CHAPTER 16
We Know

CHAPTER 17
Sisterhood of Ill Repute

CHAPTER 18
Just Amanda

CHAPTER 19
Punching Down

CHAPTER 20
Joy

CHAPTER 21
The Only Way Out Is Through

CHAPTER 22
In Bocca al Lupo

CHAPTER 23
Coraggio

CHAPTER 24
Dear Giuliano

CHAPTER 25
A New Life

CHAPTER 26
Una Vita in Gioco

CHAPTER 27
Rudy Goes Free

CHAPTER 28
An Uncertain Miracle

CHAPTER 29
Life Isn't Fair

CHAPTER 30
Preemptive Closure

CHAPTER 31
Homecoming

CHAPTER 32
Faccia a Faccia

CHAPTER 33
A Dream Deferred

CHAPTER 34
The Other Side of the Coin

CHAPTER 35
The Art of Freedom

A Benediction

CHAPTER 1
Claustrophobia

Small, enclosed spaces have always bothered me. I hid behind things or in vantage points like tree branches or the swing set when playing hide-and-seek. I never liked crawling into tight spaces, especially those with only one exit. Since losing consciousness under water when I was six, I've feared drowning—of being surrounded by enemies. I was raised in a one-story house. My sister Deanna and I shared a room. Not much time was spent indoors. I spent much of my time in our backyard or bike around town. Living near a greenbelt, Mom would take us and the dogs for daily walks into the woods, where Deanna and I would run and jump, use twigs as swords, and play Xena.

My childhood was spent outside, rain or shine. I started camping like a native. I even went backpacking on the Olympic peninsula for five days in middle school, bringing everything in and out, trekking at least five miles a day, and pitching my own tent. I helped build state park trails at twelve. Nothing felt unusual in the Pacific Northwest. I knew my house was bigger than my yard. I didn't think to not explore and immerse myself in our most fascinating natural resources—the mountains and forests.

Every day in high school, I played soccer. That early morning, frost on the grass, sun rising, adults chilly, bundled, and grumbling, drinking coffee in the stands while I stretched and ran about the wide, open field in shorts and a t-shirt was my favorite. Refreshing as a Russian ice bath. That broad area meant movement to me.

I started rock climbing in college and bouldered on weekends. I camped often with my then-boyfriend DJ, even in winter. Snow makes the world silent, which is magical. I loved listening to the trickling water, the rustle of little creatures, and the crunch of snow under my feet as we hiked through the forest to a precipice with a view of distant peaks. My camping gear was crucial, so I couldn't fathom going to Italy without it. It occupied much area! I imagined camping on Lago Trasimeno outside Perugia.

After arriving in Italy, I knew all this about myself. My expansiveness shaped every aspect of my personality. I always chose unknown anxiety over knowing misery. Because I fear change, I won't stay in an unsatisfactory relationship or career. To test how I look with a pixie cut, I'll shave off twenty inches of hair that took three years to grow.

You can imagine my reaction to four years in a little concrete box. Or for hours in an interrogation room overnight.

I had no idea that was an interrogation chamber. I was unaware of the questioning. You can remain mute. It wasn't like what you see on TV: an empty room with a table and two chairs, a one-sided mirror across the wall, and a cop slamming down a folder of crime scene images. Your words will be used against you. Two desks, file cabinets, framed certificates, and photos decorated the small, cramped workplace. I had spent hours in Meredith's room with her other roommates and friends answering questions for the inquiry over the past few days.

Officer Rita Ficarra said, "The pubblico ministero is here to see you," obviously unaware that I was folded in fetal position. The buzzing of my cell phone, my mom's attempts to call me that Ficarra blocked, and Ficarra's hand smacking me as she cried, "Remember! Remember!" kept my head ringing. The interrogation continued into the early hours of the morning as a rotating cast of officers twice my age asked me the same questions in a language I barely understood and refused my answers until I started doubting my own sanity and believing them when they said I had blacked out from trauma. Fearing thirty years in prison, I jumped out the only window they offered, unsure of my height or landing. Nothing felt like a decision. I needed to escape cyclical inquiry. I signed the statements accusing me and my partner, Raffaele Sollecito, and my supervisor, Patrick Lumumba. "You need to talk to the pubblico ministero about what you remember," Ficarra said.

"Pubblico ministero"—"public minister"—was deceptively simple to interpret, but what did it mean? A day or two after Meredith's murder, a UW representative called me. She sent her sympathy and mentioned local government authorities helping me with things. Perhaps that was her intent. I thought the pubblico ministero would save me like the mayor. Would he let me leave this tiny room?

Ficarra cleared her desk and seat. I repeated: "I'm really confused right now. This doesn't feel like remembering.

Not even looking up. "Pazienza. Memories will return."

I was saved by the pubblico ministero in the doorway. He looked like a heavier, older version of my stepdad with a round face that sat like ice cream on his suit collar. As he sat behind Ficarra's desk, he was really stern and didn't greet me. But he was calm, and after being screamed at all night, I felt hopeful we could resolve everything together.

He informed me that his name was Dr. Giuliano Mignini. We apparently met outside my house the day before. However, I had no memory of him or seeing his face, which made me doubt myself. He stated he wanted to hear me.

I rambled desperately, relieved. My mom tried to call me from Perugia. I was attempting to help, but a nightmare left me afraid and bewildered. He looked at my signed statement. "You're scared, Mr. Lumumba?"

Don't know? I'm terrified and bewildered."

He explained the document's confusing scenario and requested more details with a frown. He resisted when I tried to explain that I wasn't sure if those blurry, unconnected images were recollections or dreams. "You don't know? You must have heard. Why hit your head? "Why are you crying?" Just meek, self-deprecating complaints about being beaten and screamed at. My heart fell at his irritation and incredulity. The mayor or whatever he was didn't believe me. Trying to talk to him was like hitting a stone wall. Dejected, I quit again. I followed his advice. I signed his papers. I would comply until I saw my mom. A few hours later, she reached Perugia. We would rest in a hotel and then she would help me clean up.

Disassociated. I felt comfortable floating above and watching as they brought me into another room and told me to strip naked. I was reassured by a male doctor as he meticulously checked my neck, hands, and genitals for a photographer, looking for signs of sexual violence. They put metal cuffs on my wrists and led me down the stairs and into the parking lot, promising me that it was a formality.

Where're we going? I eventually asked.

"You are being taken to a holding place for your own protection," remarked a male officer. "Just a few days."

Early morning in Casa Circondariale Capanne. A military-uniformed man and woman led me. The man was like a half-melted candle—hunched back, drooping face, and flickering warm to cold, eager to indifferent. She looked like a vampire—pale and with flawlessly styled blood red hair. Upon removing my restraints, the man introduced himself as Vice Commandante Argirò and requested that I exclusively speak to him. ("Vice Commandante"—Vice Commander—what did that mean?) She identified herself as Agente.

Our footsteps boomed across the cement flooring of a long hallway lined on either side with doors like none I had ever seen: solid sheets of metal with no handles, just a hole, and a shuttered viewing window.

It was quiet, so I believed these doors led to unoccupied rooms. At the last door at the end of the hallway, Agente turned a massive metal key in the lock and used it as a handle to open it, revealing another steel-bar door without a handle. Agente also opened this door using the same key.

A pumpkin-orange steel bed frame, green foam mattress, and coarse wool blanket were within. Vice Commandante Argirò escorted me inside and pointed to a boxy object on the wall six feet above, wrapped in a black garbage bag and duct tape. He shouted, "Don't touch!" and "don't speak to anyone." I was alone, so this final portion confused me. He was chastising me, like he was upset at me.

As I studied his and Agente's expressions for signs of my status—was I a visitor under their protection or a nuisance under their boot? As Vice Commandante Argirò left, Agente locked both doors behind them.

The cold and quiet enveloped me. I wondered if my mom thought I was dead. I panicked and hyperventilated. Everything was a mistake. It was all my fault. What was this room? Why bars? I remembered what they promised: they were keeping me here for my safety. Just a few days. My tears put me to sleep.

It was not "a few days." To the police and prosecution, including Dr. Giuliano Mignini, I would never have left after 1,428 days.

I heard knocking the next morning, still cold and numb, lying on my bunk with my back to the barred door. It was subtle but firm, unobtrusive and undeniable, like saying "I'm here!" I hope that's okay." He was unique from the start. He knocked.

Following orders, I got up from bed. The outer metal door opened on a squarish, stubbly man with brown eyes virtually hidden by self-transitioning rectangular glasses. A casual blazer, fleece pullover with a zippered collar, jeans, and sneakers were on him. In contrast to the sharp lines and carefully plucked eyebrows of many cops and jail officials, his casual style felt almost Pacific Northwest.

Still, I approached cautiously. He probably thought I was shy, but I've never been. Shyness didn't keep me bowed and recoiled, speaking in whispers.

The little silver cross on his jacket collar revealed who or what he was.

Hi, he said, his voice like honey and sand. "Do you know Italian?"

At least I comprehended that statement. I nodded.

He introduced himself as Don Saulo. Im a priest. Im here to assist. Want to talk?

I shook my head in apology. "I'm not religious."

I told the nun in her starched gray habit who came by earlier that morning. She said I was like an animal without God.

I was astonished when the priest just laughed. "How about I have the agente bring you to my office soon? You can chat about anything."

I considered the invites to speak from police, the public ministry, and Vice Commandante Argirò, but none felt like a choice. "Okay," I said.

To be polite, he nodded farewell and carefully slid the exterior door partially closed.

Later, Agente opened the locked door and invited me. She followed as I moved down the empty hallway, now lit by the far window. I felt invisible women eyeing me from their partially closed doors.

Down the stairs, through another guarded gate, into another hallway. The tiny Don Saulo office had a low couch on the left and a tall cabinet on the right. The sunlight from the window at the end of the room illuminated the old priest at his desk facing the door. As I arrived, he looked up, thanked Agente, who closed the door, and suggested I sit in the chair across from him. I obeyed.

I forget how he broke the ice. Asking how I was doing? I only remember dripping desperation. There was a mistake. No, I did not. I shouldn't be here. Nobody believes me. No one believes me!"

He touched my hand across the table and said, "You're here for a reason." He meant that as "God is looking out for you," but I heard it as "Well, you must have done something," and I quietly chastised myself for my foolishness.

I said, "I'm innocent, but they yelled at me, and I got confused. Police are furious with me. Not listening. They don't believe me. Do you? I rambled and unraveled. I simply needed someone to believe me, not especially him.

He shielded my hand and picked his words carefully. "I believe you are… sincere," he said. Again, he meant kindness. He didn't know me or what happened, so what could he say? However, I heard it as "I believe you want to be innocent." I'm devastated. I slowly drew my hand into my lap, despondent.

No, I couldn't say anything. His sympathy ran off me like rain from a stone statue in a deserted piazza.

It took me a time to comprehend that the area I was kept in was my cell, that the outer metal door was a "blindo," and that "Agente" meant "guard." I eventually saw the red-haired lady who locked me in that first night and the other guards as one many-faced Agente. Even their interchangeability was a cage that kept messages and pleas out. God's vast distance distanced even the priest from me. No one seems reachable here. I was confined by my jail walls, linguistic barriers, and the indifference of those who kept me here.

The police or warden ordered me to be isolated for the investigation, so I had no access to common areas for my first eight months in prison. I was not isolated. First few weeks, I shared a cell with another woman. Scabs from her obsessive scratching covered her body. I don't know her prison time. Agente promised me she was a veteran when she moved me in. I imagined her traumas. Whatever they were, they irritated and confused her. Another way I felt confined was staying quiet to manage her mood swings.

Before prison, I had the invisible luxury of spending time in locations that exuded freedom—the woods, the open soccer pitch, the family summer visits to Lake Roosevelt in Eastern Washington. I frequented such areas. Nothing felt like a decision. Freedom seemed impossible now, cut off from that boundless universe.

I ran circles in the courtyard next to the chapel reserved for me whenever I could leave my cell. I skipped, jogged, and performed jumping jacks. I circled the courtyard like a dog at a fence line in the rain, feeling my blood pulse and relaxing me. And I sung. Beatles, Dido, Eagles—I sang them. I sung Christmas songs like "The Star-Spangled Banner." I sang every memorized tune. It was enough to feel my body vibrate and hear my words echo down the hallways and out beyond the prison walls, a small part of me riding the wind. Over time, I realized that my physical reality and perspective—literally—determined how free I felt. If I saw the locked door, I hyperventilated. If my perspective was the old stone tower on the hillside a few kilometers from the prison or the tiny bunnies playing in the grass below, everything changed. I always had that option. After choosing not to look at the many things boxing me in, I discovered possibilities within that concrete box I never could have imagined.

CHAPTER 2
Possessed

Books have always fascinated me. Thanks to my schoolteacher mom. Sitting on her lap and perusing pages are some of my earliest memories. I was also the kid in my homemade wizard robe standing in line at midnight to get the next Harry Potter book. I read and cuddled with a dog while not dashing around. I spent three weeks in Japan at fourteen after being obsessed with manga in middle school—Magic Knight Rayearth, Sailor Moon, Ranma Nibun-no-Ichi. Shakespeare captivated me in college. I appreciated the words and the intricate stories and memorable characters. A scene or line that evolved just so with distinct mixtures of linguistic flare and restraint, with turns of phrase that were events in themselves, gave me chills. When I was prepared for my study abroad in Perugia, I loved the Italian language, which sounded so sweet with all those vowels at the end of words. I expected to spend hours browsing Italian bookstores for "authentic" versions of Invisible Cities, The Decameron, and Pinocchio.

A dictionary was requested days after my arrest. I unintentionally ordered a beard comb and hair removing cream from the commissary list instead of deodorant and a hairbrush. I asked Agente for a washing machine to do my laundry and was sent to the bathroom bidet. Agente felt sorry for me and gave me publications other inmates threw away. Translating them by researching each term in the dictionary was tedious. After a few weeks, I reluctantly accepted that I wouldn't be coming home "in a few days" as the police had claimed. As consolation, I hoped to be placed on house arrest by my family. I finally requested a book. Agente took me to the library, a glorified closet next to the warden's office, and let me choose one book. The closet held largely Italian romance novels. The Italian masterpieces L'Amore Molesto by Elena Ferrante, Il Gattopardo by Giuseppe di Lampedusa, and I Promessi Sposi by Alessandro Manzoni were new to me. I saw an Italian copy of Harry Potter and the Goblet of Fire, which was my only good luck in a while.

I joyfully struggled through that book. I understood it even when I couldn't parse a sentence after reading it four times in English. That happened often. Every page stuck me a dozen times, especially early on. Every time, I wrote the sentence in a notebook and used the Italian-English dictionary to decipher it. Harry Potter was essential to my Italian learning.

That poor library had few volumes, but I was granted three in my cell. My family brought me books, but they didn't know what to gift me—they were reading Twilight, which I didn't like. However, University of Washington Italian professor Giuseppe Leporace allowed me to continue earning credit through independent study in those early days. I received packets of Italian poetry, parables, and short stories like Il Novellino to examine and translate into English.

I couldn't visit the school room, where an elementary school teacher volunteered once a week to teach inmates to read and write, because I was isolated. She might assist me translate one of Professor Leporace's poems. I begged Agente to let the teacher visit my cell when she could. She arrived grumpily. She laughed at me and claimed I was wasting her time when I informed her about my poem translation. Without helping me, she went. It was clear from her expression: Who are you? Poetry? Your stay is permanent.

I had three books in my cell but little else. Two shoes, five socks, two pencils, one metal plate. Every item in prison is numbered. Possession rules were illogical. We could have a camp fire with an open flame, but not nutmeg, likely because a cellblock woman tried to snort it. Bleach was allowed, but we had to wear socks when it got chilly because we couldn't wear gloves.

Besides my books, my cell's most valuable items were my family and friend photos. After months of isolation and little contact with outsiders, Capanne's world and its inhabitants became half-dreams. I would hold a picture of my mother against the wall while writing her a letter to remind myself of her realness—her personality, quirks, hobbies, voice. I tried to imagine each family member while writing. I could carry ten photos. I had a large family, so I chose ten people to imagine clearly that week. Then I had to write a "domandina"—a request form—to the warden to swap one batch of photos for another, trading this cousin for that one, letting one friend into my immediate world while another lost definition in the fuzzy strokes of memory as they were sealed back into the prison's storage locker holding all my forbidden items.

Two Italian men—local lawmaker Rocco Girlanda and his colleague Corrado Daclon—filled that storage container with books. They promoted US-Italy friendship as Italy USA Foundation representatives. They asked if I needed anything, and I responded Libri. Then my literary world exploded. Umberto Eco, Alberto Moravia, Italo Svevo, and Leonardo Sciascia were my favorite Italian authors, and Rocco and Corrado brought me as many as I could read

I could only have three books in my cell and had to ask Agente to swap them out weekly. Not sure how many novels I read in prison. Over my time at Capanne, I probably read 200 books.

Just one: Viktor Frankl's Man's Search for Meaning. My model and motivation was this book. It's Frankl's candid description of his concentration camp existence and a meditation on how others can learn from him. Frankl developed and popularized logotherapy and existential analysis to help people find meaning. His practical advise (make every moment count; find a unique vocation you can do) and his raw nerve to exist in the face of endless suffering connected with me, and still do.

The closest thing I had to a "How to Survive Prison" booklet was my black edition with gold lettering in prison. I wasn't tortured or starved like concentration camp prisoners, but my experience was similar to Frankl's and my fellow prisoners'. I was surprised upon admittance and fought with apathy while I adjusted. I detached, feeling like I was seeing myself from above. I saw how bitterness poisoned many of the women around me—prisoner and agente—but also how some "decent" agenti and prisoners resisted moral deformity by quietly finding purpose through work, caring for others, or maintaining dignity.

That sense of dignity came from Frankl's book and reading in general. Books helped me escape Capanne's cacophony and melancholy. They taught me the vocabulary I needed to survive prison and defend myself in court. They were my therapists, gurus, and pals when my real friends were across the world. They suffered the indignity of incarceration even as they represented noble things to me. Many of my prison books have missing spines, so you might spot them in my library. No hardcover books were allowed, so when my family or supporters sent me one, the cardboard cover and spine had to be cut off, leaving a wiggling bundle of pages inside its dust jacket. They were attractive despite their ugliness.

The more I spent in Capanne, the more I valued my materialistic possessions above my books and photos. Like all my possessions in that milieu, my body was out of my control. I stripped naked before and after full-body pat-downs several times a day. Others controlled my body's movement between boxes. Do you own anything if you can't select how and when to use it?

I controlled my mind—my thoughts, memories, and self-image. Even though the world was full of lies about me, my thoughts, my cares, and my worth, I strongly safeguarded these. But none of that could change or take away what I knew to be true.

Even if tangible goods seem to generate and support your inner reality, they don't. Does it delight you? Marie Kondo's "Does this pair of shoes bring me joy?" test may help you decide whether to keep or donate your possessions, but it doesn't answer the big question: How much stuff should you have, even if it all makes you happy? It's more than three books and ten photos for me, but living that spartan lifestyle changed my perspective and taught me that while food, water, and shelter are essential, true joy and peace must come from within. You can't base it on what you can hold, buy, or treasure. Nothing has that power. Life will bring surprises and disasters. Things will be lost, destroyed, or given away. You can enjoy that photo of your mother or that spineless copy of Dante's Divine Comedy without attaching delight to them. It's not paradoxical. I learnt to appreciate what I had because it could all be snatched away in an instant. I was enough after losing almost everything.

CHAPTER 3
Ikigai

She approached me first. After a year in gen-pop, my trial began, and I realized how much difficulty I was in. Our bunkmate sat cross-legged. She was eleven or twelve. Her face was freckled and hair long and knotted. Her slender, athletic torso was covered by an oversize red-and-black plaid shirt. Her vibe was questioning, and she stared at me like, What the hell are you doing here?

I couldn't answer that question satisfactorily. I had given up on home arrest and was worried about the prosecution's case. Dr. Giuliano Mignini and his colleagues created a ridiculous scenario unless you assumed Amanda was guilty. I had to establish my innocence, not just my innocence. I had no idea how.

As another inmate hissed "Infame!" from the corridor, I turned away from the small child. Snitch. I was having a bad week. I was still the oddball kid in town. Eight months in isolation meant I didn't understand prison social dynamics. As the sole American whose case was publicized by every Italian news station, Agente and prisoner continually questioned me. Even though most people ignored me, I felt lonely and paranoid.

However, the entire cell block was looking at me evilly. Some women spat at me, while others violently shoulderd me in the yard. I didn't know why until Agente threw a tabloid in my face—it had leaked that I'd informed my mom a former cellmate had harassed me by watching me wash. My mom didn't tell anyone, so jail officials taped and leaked our talk to the press.

I looked at the girl opposite me. "This will happen to you," I said. "They'll imprison you for a crime you didn't commit. When you tell your mom about the guards and prisoners harassing you, they'll spit at you and call you a snitch. Sadness awaits. You'll be alone. Nothing will make sense."

She seemed unfrightened by the news. More astonished. She appeared to ask, Wait, what? Tell me more.

She started visiting me often, always in my cell alone. Never in the yard or with others. She came from soccer, gymnastics, Pokémon, and Harry Potter. Her free spirit spoke of easy friendships, family dinners, and climbing trees. Although she sat across from me, she couldn't see my phone and asked me to explain. I told her about my window view of the cypress trees, the gristle they served us twice a day, and the locked door I couldn't abide.

She spoke little. I mostly talked to her about my challenges and what was coming, encouraging her she would get through it. The bigness of it all—feeling confined and unsafe day after day—was more than just a guard refusing to give me the food my family provided on visitation day or a cellmate accusing me of taking her tobacco (I don't smoke). "You'll survive," I said.

How?

"I don't know how, but you will. I assure you."

Okay, I suppose. Always cautiously optimistic.

As pleased as I was to join gen-pop, sharing a cell with four other women and walking the yard daily had drawbacks. Mostly because I was different. Being the only American and "famous" was bad. My face appeared on TV screens when game shows and soap operas weren't on, along with scandalous conjecture about drug-addled sex-fiend Foxy Knoxy. I would have done anything to erase that media publicity. However unfavorable the attention, the other women, many of whom had been overlooked or forgotten by society and felt even more neglected and forgotten in prison, were jealous. This made me a target.

I was one of the few prisoners who received mail and visitors daily, which didn't help. I received so much mail—not just from family and friends, but from strangers with marriage proposals and death threats—that the agenti grumbled about how long it took them to open and inspect it. My family sometimes fed and clothed me. I rapidly learnt to share or offer my cellmates everything. They needed it more than I did and had less cause to despise me.

The women's block at Capanne jail saw occasional violence. I saw women punch each other in the face. My cellmate tore my journal because she thought I was writing about her. One day, while walking with a cellmate, or concellina—an Italian phrase I devised that Don Saulo liked clever—another woman raced up behind us in the yard. I saw her massaging her palms in frantic anticipation. It was terrible. She mashed glue from a stick into her palms. She jumped on the woman next to me and ripped her hair in chaos. I froze, and my legs gave out. Another cellmate rescued me.

When that little girl came to me later that day, I was too horrified by the violence to say anything. Instead, Mom told me I was tough: You hurt your foot playing soccer and kept playing! She didn't know me as

I did. She knew me, not my transformation. As her older sister, I gave her the advice and reassurance I needed now. She couldn't know that sometimes I lied when I said she'd live.

I shrank into myself when she wasn't there, despite how huge I was for her. I initially survived by wearing earplugs and reading. Most of my fellow convicts had trauma, mental illness, and drug addiction. They had trouble controlling emotions and impulses. In cramped surroundings, we rationally saw each other as threats and competitors for precious resources. Being forced to adapt to an environment that rewarded violence and penalized weakness outweighed any benefits from theoretical beekeeping or other rehabilitation initiatives. Beekeeping without bees?

As my Italian improved and the others saw I wasn't a threat, I saw the prison marketplace of time and energy. Like black-market FedEx, Sabrina worked in commissary. She traded notes, CDs, and cigarettes between cells. We could cook, but we had terrible ingredients, so it was helpful to be friends with Angela, who worked in the kitchen and had garlic cloves and, if you were lucky, rosemary sprigs.

What about you? You help how? younger self asked. The women around me had various needs. They required dentistry. I had all my teeth, unlike other convicts. They needed love. I was one of few with frequent guests. They required legal aid. One of the few with a lawyer on my side. I couldn't bring their relatives, treat their ailments, or give them legal counsel, but I recognized I could help since I could read and write. Many women around me were illiterate. A cellmate learned to read the analog clock from me. While explaining how distant my home was, I was surprised to learn she didn't know the world was a sphere.

Most evenings, I visited Nigerian women who called me "America." They set the table before I arrived. They always brought me a pear juice box, my favorite. I then translated their court paperwork, boyfriend letters, and innuendo-filled responses from Pidgin English from the King James Bible into appropriate Italian.

Even Agente requested my assistance. Language didn't matter. I helped a Chinese woman communicate a medical issue to the doctor. I stumbled through a Chinese-English dictionary my family gave me (I'm a language nerd) and translated from Chinese to English to Italian.

"Looking at what you have to offer and what the women around you need will help you find your place," I told my younger self. "The unofficial prison translator and scribe will be you."

Will that protect me?

"Safe as you can be," I said. "But it will also feel good."

It was true. Literacy gave me social capital to negotiate prison life safer. Helping these women gave me meaning. Not merely languishing. In the cellblock's poor society, I contributed. My prison hustle taught me that selfishness and selflessness are compatible. Every Venn diagram has a sliver where what serves you and others overlaps. Ikigai is the Japanese word for this. It combines your talent, enthusiasm, world need, and income. Always loved languages, I studied Italian in Perugia with the goal of becoming a translator. Translating court paperwork and love letters in prison wasn't what I expected, but it fulfilled all four requirements. In prison, I got juice boxes, safety, and respect for doing something I liked, was good at, and was sorely needed in my community.

"Ikigai" means "reason for being." We all have one, and from my experience, you can discover it even in the worst situations. We focus on two of the four circles—talent and pay—in the West, frequently only the latter. Got passion? Just a hobby. What's global good? A business, not a charity! But the latter one is crucial since kindness is more gratifying than money. It gave me energy and purpose.

Kindness is self-serving. I instinctively recognized this as a kid. It feels fantastic and returns unexpectedly. My kitchen-worker friend Laura baked me a chocolate cake for my 23rd birthday, even though I had ceased celebrating my birthday in prison. Before Sabrina slipped the illegal treat through my cell bars with a wink, it passed through several hands in a waste bag. Smashed and gooey, it was fantastic.

After prison, I never saw my younger self again. I was excited to see her smiling at me in my mom's photo albums, but I never felt like she was in my cell, so real I could smell the dirt under her fingernails, the sweat on her flannel from endless tag games, and the peanut butter on her breath.

In those moments, I might have wanted the thirty-five-year-old me to travel back in time and tell the bewildered, terrified twenty-year-old sitting in front of her that I would survive the nightmare. However, without that future confidence, I could only repay twelve-year-old myself. That lifted my existential crises and put it in front of me so I could evaluate and learn from it. Looking at my situation, at what I could control and what I couldn't, gave me the strength to promise my younger self, even though it seemed like a lie: You will survive. You will!

I now know it was true. Yes, I survived. Got through it. I learned. Thanks to her visits. She showed me I could help others even when I couldn't.

"Why came you here?" When she initially appeared, I asked. She stared at me as if the answer were so apparent that the question astonished her.

You needed me.

CHAPTER 4
Tutto Fa Brodo

I like food. Growing up, my family considered me a bottomless hole. I would get the biggest hamburger, eat as many waffles as possible, and suck every drop of sauce off a platter. Due to my unusual activity, I had a big appetite. I was a hyperactive 12-year-old playing three sports and running about.

Consuming food is different from cooking. Food came from boxes or freezers at my dad's place. Many Hamburger Helper and Costco hot dogs were eaten. Cooking at my mom's place was easy: steam rice, sauté chicken, season with lemon pepper. Mom was thrilled to find a recipe for orzo salad with peppers, olives, and tomatoes. Oma's house was where I ate most. Oma cooked German food constantly. She occasionally made spaghetti, but it was terrible—mushy noodles, canned sauce. Germans aren't pasta experts. Since Oma usually had too much food, I took leftovers to school and ate lentil stew with ham hock while other kids ate ham and cheese sandwiches. My students thought my food looked terrible, but I enjoyed eating it in front of them to show how good it was. German food's savory and pickly deliciousness was absent.

Though I helped Oma make rouladen at Christmas—beef packed with pickles and onions and topped with gravy— I rarely cooked as a child or young adult. Early in college, I lived on Thai takeaway and cheap sushi. I remembered how amazing real Italian cuisine was from a family trip to Rome when I was 14, and as I prepared for my semester abroad, salivating over handmade pizza, I had no idea how much my relationship with food would change.

I entered Italy open-mouthed. I added the freshest mozzarella and ripest tomatoes. The simple ingredients were so good I didn't cook. This was one of my favorite things about Italy. Italians are serious about food—cooking, eating, and forming their social environment around it. Within five weeks, my gastronomic world changed. At least till my arrest.

I often hear, half-jokingly, "Hey, at least the prison food must have been better in Italy!" If someone chooses an Italian restaurant for dinner, I say, "Sorry, you're probably sick of it!" However, I didn't eat Italian food for four years. I ate prison cuisine. Prison cuisine is prison food, including Capanne.

Hot drinks were served for breakfast every day. I normally drank instant coffee, which tasted like toast but not horrible. Lunch and dinner were served by handing your metal plate through a slit in the locked door and slopping on starch, veggies, and meat. Olive oil-drizzled spaghetti was the carbohydrate. I rarely ate it. Though I adore vegetables, jail food was tasteless and overcooked. Boiling carrots. Boiling spinach. A boiled potato. Layers of starch. Protein was frequently cartilage rather than meat, and I rarely knew its source. I never touched it.

As expected, I dropped weight. I got skinny without much space or food. I believed my body reflected my mentality. I'd always eaten and moved with gusto, but suddenly I didn't.

We sometimes got only men's prison leftovers. Food arrived chilly, but it was the same. Once, they ran out of food and gave us bread. But we could buy commissary food. I lived off precooked lentil pouches when the food was too bad. We could also cook a little. We could buy oil and spices.

My cellmates and I decided to create gnocchi from our lunches of boiled potatoes. Blankly, I watched. Unsure how to make gnocchi? I could only microwave a Hot Pocket, but I wanted to learn. It was easy to make gnocchi, but it took time. We made dough by mashing potatoes, kneading them with egg and flour, and pressing them in our palms with a thumb. A brief boil, olive oil, and salt—mwah! They were tasty.

I learned to cook this way. My cellmates and I made something tasty from the prison's bad components. We could buy flour and yeast to make pizza dough. But how to implement? Naturally, with a broomstick. Our pizza oven was a camp fire pot. I discovered I like ingredients I never would have bought in Seattle. I like raw fennel instead of boiled greens as the vegetable of the day. I turned commissary-bought raw fennel into a salad with olives and oranges. However, these delightful moments were rare. I missed eating, especially sushi. It was my fantasy. More than the food, I dreamed of the family gatherings I missed, where everyone gathered for company and food. I knew Oma lit a candle at supper to represent me back home.

On good days, I felt like that candle—wavering, frail, yet dazzling. Prison taught me that I could find warmth in a cage, that a little work, inventiveness, and modest ingredients could produce a good dinner, and to be grateful.

In Italian, "tutto fa brodo" means everything produces broth. Vegetable peels, chicken bones, and fish skins are boiled to make broth. Wasted materials become the foundation of your creativity. Everything matters and has a purpose.

Capanne was filled of trash. Sabrina, the 18-year-old crook, vividly remembered pickpocketing visitors and snatching Vespas for an afternoon thrill. Antonia, the thirty-year-old lunatic who drank rotten milk and whispered about becoming God. Maria, the stay-at-home mother who hid cocaine for the mafia and crocheted nonstop. Rosa, the 28-year-old model sent to prison for murdering her chain-smoking, voracious reader boyfriend. Fulvio, the drug-dealing trans man who brazenly flirted with every gorgeous cellblock lady.

We made what kind of broth?

I often felt disconnected from my surroundings. I didn't smoke, gossip, watch soaps, or argue. I craved solitude most of the time. I couldn't belong, and I couldn't relate to others' or their experiences all too often.

So Maria taught me to make gnocchi. Sabrina taught me belly dancing. Rosa loaned me her Fabri Fibra CD to interpret poems. Fulvio amused me. Antonia was generally harmless and trying her best. For better or worse, I was exposed to the humanity of the women incarcerated in Capanne, women who had committed minor and serious crimes and struggled with mental illness, impulse control, and emotional instability.

They were not my pals. I suppose they were my peers because we were all simmering in the same pot. We all experienced being rejected. We all experienced life without opportunity and purpose. Every day, while we rub shoulders and watched our lives slip away, we found new opportunities and purposes in each other, even if it was as simple as shaking boiling milk in an empty two-liter water bottle till it foamed. Like many jail luxuries, brewing a cappuccino at siesta was only worthwhile if the whole cell was around the percolator.

We were separated like cafeteria tray dividers when we slipped our plates through the bars to get our slop. We might have wanted those bits of food like wary animals. But breaking bread meant resistance and freedom. It let us create a new family for a supper.

CHAPTER 5
Desire

Lynne was grumpy when she arrived at Capanne. She paced the yard alone, head bowed and shoulders strained. This was typical for transfers. Each prison has a delicate ecosystem, so being uprooted and transplanted without warning was shocking and scary. I assessed her—petite, slight belly, unkempt hair. She closed in on herself, so I figured she'd only lash out when cornered. She didn't threaten me.

After watching me exercise around the yard every day, Lenny got up the nerve to say hello. I was cautiously pleasant because as the "famous one," I didn't trust extra attention. However, I didn't mind her walking with me around the perimeter, the cement walls so high I could only see the sky. She instantly revealed that she was a lesbian and asked if I was uncomfortable. "Of course not," I answered. At my Catholic high school, I helped form the gay–straight alliance. Lenny told me Italians were still judgmental and closed-minded. My sympathies. I was teased for being gay at fourteen. I became an ally because of that.

For a few weeks, I let Lenny borrow my CD player and CDs. She preferred Norah Jones and Dido. I taught her chess. When she worked as a janitor, she stopped by my cell for coffee and chats on breaks. I knew Lenny enjoyed our time together because she had no one else. I received several letters a day and was visited weekly by one of my parents. All my touchstones were in the free world. Lenny's only link was becoming me. I knew where that might lead after being in long enough. I fretted about whether she liked me or Foxy Knoxy.

Formerly a soccer nickname. On the diamond, I was defense first. I was good at preying on the ball. The term stayed because I knew it was cheeky. It was a thirteen-year-old girls' team. I had no idea a dumb nickname would curse me.

The media pounced on "Foxy Knoxy" after finding my abandoned MySpace profile. "Foxy Knoxy" became "Volpe Cattiva"—wicked fox—in Italian, bolstering my sexual deviant image.

My prosecutor, Dr. Giuliano Mignini, lied about this guy in court. In his closing remarks, he said Amanda likely aggressively slammed Meredith against the wall, hurting her neck, to vent her wrath. As Amanda forced her fingers under Meredith's chin, Raffaele seized her hair from behind, immobilizing her. Rudy tried to gain Amanda's love as Raffaele defended his boyfriend status. Poor Meredith was caught in the middle. She fell. They undressed her. The assault became a sex game. Meredith presumably kneeled once her jeans were taken off. Amanda held the knife and watched Raffaele and Rudy grope and abuse her companion. Amanda, enraged with Meredith for criticizing her casual promiscuity, may have called her a prude, ridiculed her, and stated, "You're such a goody two-shoes." We'll demonstrate. We'll make you have sex!"

This narrative fueled the global media's portrayal of me as a sex-crazed femme fatale.

I sought to disappear in Capanne. Quiet and withdrawn. I wore baggy sweats. All my hair was cut. I sometimes thought about when the Scarecrow Video counterman asked me to pose for a "tasteful, softcore" amateur porn film at nineteen. "No sex! Just showering!" I was offered $2,000. I was taking full classes and working two part-time jobs to save for my study abroad. I winced at what the newspapers and Dr. Giuliano Mignini would have done if I did it.

I tried to disappear, but failed. Initially, I endured mandatory evening visits with Vice Commandante Argirò for two weeks. In a private office, he praised my size, face, and "blond" hair. He asked me about my undergarments and sex life and propositioned me. After months, a male agente cornered me in a toilet on July 4, days before my twenty-first birthday, grabbed me around the waist, and tried to kiss me.

Raffaele wrote me letters from his incarceration, encouraging me we will get through this. He even dropped the L-bomb, but I wasn't sure if Italians used "love" more lightly. After one week together, our worlds were turned upside down. I was moved, but I didn't want a love relationship. Even Raffaele's earnest need made me shudder to be desired. I told him that our intimate relationship before we were arrested was over. Romance didn't help me through this.

Many of my fellow convicts relied on romance. Prison makes women more likely to have experienced poverty, mental illness, and abuse, and it strains and weakens their family bonds. So they form a family within.

Most detainees were Italian, Nigerian or Romani and belonged to prison social organizations. (I just acquired this polite term after release. Romani people I met called each other "zingare," gypsies. Prisoners established cliques, families, partnerships. Nigerians called each other "Mama" and "Daughter" and their sons' names. Mama Daniel. Mom Lucas. Romani called each other "cousin." As the only

American, I wasn't in any group. That made me see society like an anthropological. And I saw that women often formed personal, non-sexual relationships that had romance elements.

Inmates had crushes. The friendship boundaries slipped. They exchanged love messages and gifts like flower drawings and crocheted CD satchels. When her partner became too familiar with other inmates, one half of a notoriously volatile relationship sulked and stared. There were tearful breakups and fistfights between new and old lovers. Many couples acted like star-crossed teenagers, but others were as self-contained as if they had been married for twenty years.

I realized something was up when Lenny asked to hold my hand and said, "I can do things for you that no man can." When I told her I wasn't interested, she thought I was playing hard to get. She kissed me one day unexpectedly. I didn't feel threatened, but it was unwelcome, and I told her we couldn't be friends since she didn't respect my limits. After that, tension rose. Lenny pouted outside my cell during a break from work, saying I was exaggerating. My relief came when she was released, but she often wrote to me and sent CDs with "Love always,Lenny" on the inside jacket. I didn't reply.

I regretted my coldness toward her. She wasn't just attempting to make me "gay for the stay"—a word that shows a complete misunderstanding of prison relationships. People create romantic relationships for several reasons. Sex isn't always first, main, or vital. We all need companionship, closeness, care, someone to be vulnerable with, someone to touch, and someone to share our fears, anxieties, hopes, and dreams. An setting designed to humiliate, isolate, and punish makes these requirements even more important. Prison is terrible because it denies people their strongest, finest instinct—the need to connect—essential for their sanity and life.

I steadily explored my sexuality in prison, but I didn't discover emotional or sexual intimacy with other convicts. I found it challenging and significant. I had to overcome shame to consider it.

My childhood humiliation and puritan American society caused my mom to cover her ears when I asked about sex as a teenager. In my early college years, the double standard that made sexually active guys players and women sluts was low-key misogyny. Naturally, I was slut-shamed during my murder trial. That first month in Perugia sparked my interest in sex and relationships. Italy, after all. I read my mom's Under the Tuscan Sun. I wasn't coming to Italy for the unexpected encounter of a lifetime, but I looked forward to it like in movies. Like Amélie, I imagined riding a Vespa with my lovely sweetheart, holding his waist. But it didn't go as planned. One young man I met on a train to Florence gave me oral herpes, while another introduced me to the Bellini but was hard in bed. I met Raffaele, my young, attractive dream boyfriend, but that didn't go as planned either.

Looking back, I'm surprised that I rediscover my sexuality when my privacy was most violated and I was shamed and reviled more than most people would ever be. Maybe it makes sense since sexual closeness involves weakness, and I had never been so vulnerable.

Additionally, intimacy is inevitable. Like language, it's essential to adulthood, and like food and water, we'll do anything for a bite. The slaughter of gay individuals in Iran or the centuries of women diagnosed with "female hysteria," put into mad asylums, and hysterectomies for sexual desire come to mind.

Our right to suppress others' consensual sexuality. How cruel and senseless to judge and shame each other. How cruel we are to women seeking intimacy.

I was conscious that I was maturing as a sexual woman in an unbelievable misogynistic mess. I'm still shocked by how extreme the misogyny in my trials was, even though many writers have noted it. No one mentioned Rudy Guede's sexual depravity for viciously raping Meredith. Instead, my claimed sexual deviancy sparked eight years of trials and tabloid tales.

During it, I just dimly realized a sex double standard. I hadn't read about how common it was for male violence to be treated as normal and inevitable in sex crimes, so much so that a female victim is often blamed for dressing too provocatively, as if the man's uncontrollable lust was a known factor every woman should work around to avoid being raped.

I had a vague idea of the magnitude and history of misogyny and how my circumstance was not unique. But I saw clearly how my sexuality was being used against me, how it was being twisted to demonize me, how I was loathed as a killer and a sexually active woman.

Meredith's buddy was called on the witness by Dr. Giuliano Mignini to testify about the vibrator in my toiletry bag. Mignini asked, "And when Meredith told you about this and you saw it... was Meredith angry with Amanda?"

The bright pink, five-inch vibrator resembled a bunny. My best friend in Seattle gave it as a joke. I have only tried it once or twice unsuccessfully.

"Not really," Meredith's friend said. It seemed odd to her more than anything else."

Next morning's tabloid headline: Dead girl feared Knoxy's sex toy.

Under a glossy Italian leather boot, my sexual spark was crushed like a cigarette. It seemed reasonable for me to repress and loathe my sexuality because of what had occurred to me. But I just knew it was fine. Perhaps because my sexuality was accentuated and perverted, I recognized how ridiculous the hatred was. I was not disliked; my prosecutor and the media constructed a sick, filthy fantasy. Ironically, the gap between that fantasy and myself confirmed my normal and healthy sexuality. The creators of this warped fantasy were disturbed. This knowledge helped me revive my sexuality.

I waited for my cellmates to sleep. I walked silently, without even rustling a blanket. My clumsiness prevented me from orgasming before the agente arrived. Every 15 minutes, they opened the small cell windows to see inside. Like most things in life, limitations can be useful. The agente rotation made me discover my body and mental space. That brief pleasure made my body feel like mine again, but more importantly, defiant. I was recovering something natural, nutritious, and delicious that my prosecutor had utilized to prove my immorality. He was wrong, the tabloids were wrong, and letting all that distance me from my body would be just another thing they stole from me.

CHAPTER 6
Amicus Fidelis Protectio Fortis

GOD IS NULL. Down deep I realized this when Mom's Catholic boyfriend chased me across the house with rage. I was five and had fought his three- or four-year-old son. I hid in the closet, but my boyfriend found me and spanked me across his knee. Mom jumped in to save me after my first scream—she didn't believe in corporal punishment. I can still see the small, golden cross hanging from his neck, swaying gently with each smack, but I may have imagined that.

Some things about my partner I liked. I joined his clown ensemble and wore a clown outfit in parades. He gave us Tang and played Elton John's "Crocodile Rock" loudly for a dance party. I disliked that dad forced us to church every Sunday. When he left, it was just me, my sister, and Mom again. Years later, Mom told me that he was urging her to enroll Deanna and me in catechism courses to make our family more religious.

My mother taught elementary school, but by high school, I was considering private schools, even though we couldn't afford them. Seattle Prep, a Jesuit high school across town, was the only place I could learn Japanese. I adored Pokémon cards, anime, and comics. Mom helped me and provided financial aid since she valued a good education. I didn't expect to have religion class and mass at school.

We studied several theologies in religion class, but we mostly read Christian writings. We had to write essays about how religion affected us. Most of my classmates went to Catholic primary and intermediate schools and swam in this water. But I often felt breathless. Everyone assumed God exists, is benevolent, and has a plan for you, me, and everyone. I didn't know why this was wrong until prison, but I felt it. This was the first time I had to declare my beliefs, so I became agnostic to stop people from inquiring about God. My rebellion showed in religion class, when I wrote paganism essays. Instead of believing in Wicca, I found it fascinating and amusing. Years later, I met West Memphis Three member Damien Echols—we were released from prison days apart. He was convicted and executed for his Wicca interest, which portrayed him as a demon worshiper. Thank god my prosecutors didn't find my religion class essays! My teacher liked my writing, gave me good scores, and said every good Christian is a good pagan.

My religious relationship soured after my incarceration. Italy is a Catholic nation, therefore religion permeates practically every facet of life, including justice. The day I was brought into court for preliminary hearings eight months into my sentence, that became painfully evident. A big wall crucifix showed Christ's lifeless figure peering over the judge's shoulder. As my trial began, I realized how much the Catholic perspective would determine my fate.

At twenty, I was a typical American girl. Perhaps I was sheltered. I had intercourse with seven individuals in my life, but the court and press portrayed that as the number I had in Perugia in my short weeks.

In her early 20s, Meredith was normal. She had several boyfriends. Like me, she was casually dating an Italian boy in Perugia. As she and Giacomo became amorous, she asked for a condom without shame. As college girls, we were ordinary, being more naïve than "girls gone wild." Meredith's sexuality was erased while mine was exaggerated and perverted into deviancy. I was the harlot, she the virgin.

Definitely not an accident. Mary and Mary, the Madonna and the whore, the virgin and the prostitute, are the Bible's most significant female roles. Archetypes resonated with jurors, judges, and the world. Their roles were in a good-evil fantasy. Making Meredith the ideal saint made it simpler to portray myself as pure evil, the ultimate sinner. It harmed us both.

After watching this, some family members suggested I wear a cross to court. Like me, they realized that appearances mattered more than the truth and that my fate might rely on whether I was a good Catholic girl. I refused to lie. I didn't believe in God and wouldn't lie. I was naively sure that telling the truth would solve the problem and reveal my true self. That failed. I wore my stepmom's Beatles blouse, "All you need is love," to court on Valentine's Day. I imagined wearing a Christmas sweater on Christmas. I was further branded a strange, twisted psychopath. Whatever I did, the prosecution and media saw it as proof of guilt. If I spotted my family across the courtroom—one of the rare occasions I was allowed to see them—and smiled to express my survival, As an attention whore, I was "smiling for the cameras." If I didn't grin, I seemed cold and calculated. Not just the prison cell made me feel stuck, but this idea that no matter what I did, my life spun out of control and my prospects of ever being free dwindled.

You can imagine my reaction to the concept that this was God's design. There's a reason you're here, Don Saulo told me the first day we spoke. I couldn't hear him. He heard me, physically. He heard me singing in my cell or in the small courtyard where I could stretch my legs while alone.

His rounds of checking in on the cellblock's women had him stopping at my cell door every morning for weeks. He kept inviting me to his office to chat each time he stopped by. Day after day, I rejected him. After my first visit, I realized the priest couldn't assist. Eventually, he inquired if I played instruments. I informed him, "I used to play guitar before I was stuck in here."

He said, "I have a guitar!" You may play it at mass. You can practice at my office."

I didn't like mass, but it was a chance to leave my cell and play the guitar—a small reminder of my life before this nightmare. So began our musical relationship. Once or twice a week, I spent an hour in Don Saulo's office practicing hymns on the guitar, then played and sang them during Saturday mass.

The chapel was the prison's best room. The plexiglass and bars on one wall exposed a tiny garden with natural light. Don Saulo gave his homilies in a wood-paneled alcove with a podium in front of the basic wooden pews, while I played hymns beneath images of Jesus and the Virgin Mary. Other detainees sang along, thrilled to be there. The atmosphere was sometimes celebratory. I warmed to Don Saulo during those weekly masses because it was a pleasant, inviting, and meditative sanctuary in the prison.

I played more than hymns in his office. Don Saulo let me play whatever I wanted in his office throughout the months. He listened and did paperwork as I played Beatles. After discovering my passion of languages, Dad taught me Latin expressions like "Credo ut intelligam" (I believe so that I may understand) and "Amicus fidelis protectio fortis" (A devoted friend is a solid shelter). I requested that he teach me piano fingering while listening to a CD. Back in my cell, I taped some paper together and drew a piano keyboard from memory. So I practiced on my paper piano with headphones. Like Poe's raven, my cellmate could only hear my tap tap tapping and not the music. I learned to tap gently on my paper piano and survived the week until I could visit Don Saulo's office.

Don Saulo was oddly soft and firm, harsh and delicate. Kung Fu Panda, which he brought in for one of the occasional education room movie screenings, left him bawling. He was also very rigorous. However empathetic, his honesty was always unwavering. My verdict date approached, and I needed that energy. I spent as much time as possible in his office. I enjoyed mass. Still, I needed consolation, not priestly care. Without my knowledge, Don Saulo became my best friend.

I acquired a blind spot since I was allergic to religion and dependent on religious ideas during my trial. Before I saw him, Don Saulo had settled in that blind area for about two years. He held my hand in his office after my trial, anticipating the decision, exactly as he did when I met him. As he did so, I probed the wound he left, the pain of what he had said in our first chat, that he did not know if I was innocent but believed I was sincere. No more sting. That sentence no longer felt dismissive. I suddenly perceived it as hard-edged compassion. This man respected me enough to tell me the truth.

CHAPTER 7
Tunnels

I had my first insight the day after my murder conviction. I had no idea what an epiphany felt like, but it was cold like a breeze caressing the back of the neck and raising your hairs. I realized something deep down that I hadn't understood before, and I spent months trying to figure out its consequences, like watching ripples in a pool.

I silently swept a cellblock corridor during my shift, thinking "colpevole," guilty. A fellow agente said, "Poor thing." She doesn't get it." They thought I hadn't realized I'd be confined in this spot for 26 years because I wasn't crying.

Since I was contemplating my enlightenment, I was quiet. It was this: I was not longing for my life back, as I had thought for two years. Not a lost student ready to go home. Prison was my home. I felt trapped between my life (the one I should have been leading) and a murderer's. I wasn't. Never was. The conviction, punishment, and prison were my life. I should have lived no other life. The only thing before me was my life.

In my first two years of prison, I believed my mom that there was a light at the end. That the truth would prevail and the judge and jury would recognize how ludicrous this matter was. I could not see a light in that long tunnel ahead.

Mom struggled to be positive. Despite being longer than expected, we would all pass through the tunnel and emerge. Despite my efforts, I couldn't see it. I believed the truth would liberate me. It was wrong, I realized. In my first trial, the truth didn't help. My appeal should do so, why?

Epiphany felt neutral. Simply true. Clarity was the sensation. My life sucked. Uncommitted crimes got me imprisoned. I'd spend my greatest years in prison. Love, children, and a profession were unlikely for me. Trapped in concrete walls with damaged people, many of whom were dangerous, my world would be so narrow. In spite of their best efforts to keep connected, my loved ones were on their own journeys going in various ways, and this life would isolate me from them.

I didn't realize until that moment that my life was mine, no matter how small, cruel, sad, and unfair. Mine to define and live well. Life was no longer awaited. There was only life now.

I had my epiphany alone. I couldn't make it clear to my mom, and she couldn't hear me. My mom and I fought differently. Her goal was to save me. I aimed to survive. I knew I couldn't go into that black tunnel without gasping. I had to imagine life in the dark to stop searching for a light I didn't see. My parents refused to accept what I had just understood. It was my life. She assumed I was depressed and giving up. She needed me to survive till she saved me. But I realized I would only survive if I finally recognized that I was living my life, whether I was proved innocent and liberated or not.

I imagined different realities. What if Rudy Guede killed me that night at home? If I was acquitted and released in five years? In ten? What if I served my sentence and returned home in my late 40s, physically and mentally broken? If I committed suicide?

The prison put me on suicide watch after my conviction. I went to a smaller cell with one cellmate, and Agente watched me 24/7. I wasn't sure if that was usual practice for the weeks after a heavy sentence or a specific measure for me given the intense media coverage. Perhaps they detected something in my demeanor—the way I couldn't look people in the eyes, how I held my body—that conveyed what I was thinking. Because I thought.

Everyone knew the methods. My cellblockmate tried to consume plastic pen fragments. A men's wing resident used his stove and a plastic bag to asphyxiate himself. Bedsheets can be used to hang yourself. I even thought I could kill myself by hitting my head against the bedframe in the appropriate way.

Each strategy was vividly visualized. How long before the internal bleeding was noticed if I swallowed plastic pen shards? Can they save me in surgery? If assigned sanitation duty, I could receive bleach from the cleaning cart, but how much would I need to drink? Could they pump my stomach before it worked? Hanging was more reliable, but the choking, writhing, and despair were awful.

I decided to slit my wrists. I could use a broken plastic pen. I turned on the shower as hot as possible. After waiting for my cellmates in the yard, I would lie down, make two fast vertical slits, and let the water slowly drain my life.

That appeared calm. Not messy. It was likely to succeed.

Why did I not? I knew my family, especially my mom, would suffer. I knew she would have swapped places with me instantly and would never forgive herself if I died alone. Her pain was too great, and I couldn't add to it. Second, even though I was terrified of decades in prison, I couldn't accept it. Like Meredith, I didn't deserve to die or be in this cell. My stubbornness stopped me. I never considered changing my name when I left for the same reason. My name was fine; the world had tarnished it with killer, harlot, and psychopath. If I killed myself, those lies would win. Even though I doubted the truth would save me, I treasured it. For myself, Meredith, and principle. Most importantly, I made an unconscious choice when I first fantasized about death. A life choice.

I vividly imagined all those alternative futures so they no longer felt like shadows from my unconscious dreams. As they became clear in my mind, I could release them one by one. In hindsight, that choice seems obvious, but staying alive is part of my constitution—another reason I'm lucky.

Before this moment, before seriously considering what it would mean to end my life, before standing there as a critic in front of my corpse, giving notes on the method's reliability, the anticipated pain, the mess, life had been an unconscious, unexamined habit—the thing I did when I wasn't doing anything. Living became an active choice every morning. To be or not. To suffer or kill myself to fight that sea of worries. I chose pain. That decision made me accountable for my life. Although others put me in that cell, sent me death threats, and ruined my calm, anonymous life, I chose to accept it or take the emergency exit. If it was my choice, blaming the world was pointless. Realizing that helped me accept my existence and find a way to fill it with beauty, love, and knowledge to shine the fragile light of truth in that long, dark tunnel. I wondered: how do I make this life worthwhile?

I couldn't address the broader question. There was a lesser question: how can I make today worth living? I could repeat my answer. Totally under my control. I did that. I circled the small courtyard endlessly—concrete walls, concrete floor, no grass growing through cracks. I did thousands of sit-ups on my bunk, feet under the metal bar at the end. I wrote messages to my family while viewing images on the small table facing the wall. I read one book after another with my earphones to block out the prison's clanking doors, yelling, and Italian soap operas.

These tiny achievements made the day worthwhile. I wasn't sure if these were enough to make life worthwhile, but I was interested.

I realized the light was inside me, not at the end of the tunnel. It showed me that the tunnel was never a good metaphor for my circumstances. It depicts a straight, unchanging path with a light at the end to aim for in the darkness. It implies that things will remain unchanged till you cross.

But life is different. Nothing remains constant. All is uncertain. Neither joy nor grief is constant. No credit for this insight. Ancient wisdom rediscovered again. The ninth-century Chinese poet Han Shan wrote:

"Once you realize this floating life is the perfect mirage of change,

it's breathtaking—this wild joy at wandering boundless and free."

Recognizing the impermanence of our situations relieves the feeling of being imprisoned in your life and reminds us to cherish our valuable times. This too shall pass—medieval Persian poets express this thought.

I understood that the tunnel I believed I was in was not endless as one day blended into the next in an existentially draining way. My situation didn't change much—two hours of yard time in the morning, soggy pasta for dinner, one ten-minute phone call on Fridays—but my inner experience did. The "tunnel" constantly changed shape. There was no night and day. No time in the future would be perfect. That misguided goal hindered me from being okay now.

It was hard, even terrible, to lower my goals and dreams. Letting rid of that bright, brilliant light at the end of the tunnel meant giving up the answer to all my problems. The light I lit for myself during that time was dim. Because I knew that distant light wasn't real, I was able to cope and even thrive during that crisis. Like everything in the future, it was my imagination. Even if faulty, the moment was all there was.

I woke up sad, spent the day sad, and went to bed sad, but it wasn't frantic misery. I was free to perceive reality, however sad, therefore it was a melancholy with vitality beneath the surface. With no direction and only my intuitive sense of balance, I gently walked a tightrope across a bottomless hazy abyss. Despite my freedom and legal vindication, I'm still walking that tightrope. Abyss is always there. Whoever who peered into it, like me, knows the peculiar comfort of bearing it.

CHAPTER 8
Tapestries

Don Saulo never stopped giving me priestly counsel, but our chats became more philosophical after my conviction. Women in religious doctrine, vegetarianism, homosexual marriage, adoption, and life after death were discussed. We had numerous civil disagreements. Don Saulo accepted my doubts.

He told me, "God is weaving a glorious tapestry." "Your life, mine, and all the joy and suffering in the world are part of this tapestry. Earthly viewers can only perceive the ragged ends and tangles. We must believe the tapestry is lovely and that we shall view it as God does in paradise.

That still seemed wrong. I couldn't believe God's plan included my friend's murder, my family's separation, and my decades in prison. I followed Don Saulo's stark honesty: "I think God is just a comforting story we tell ourselves to feel better because sometimes life is cruel and unfair." The sad actions of mortal men—Meredith's killer, Rudy Guede, and my prosecutor—seemed to me to be the only explanation. I'm in prison for a purpose. God didn't intend it. Dr. Giuliano Mignini.

As usual, Don Saulo believed. "Reality can only exist as an expression of love," he said, "because someone loved it into being. While you may not believe, praying doesn't hurt. Maybe someone loves you—pray to him."

It was not his first time saying this. I sought to understand Don Saulo's religious philosophy. Even then, I didn't understand. Why pray if you believe in God and his plan? Why do I see many convicts pray to God for relief, release, money, and cigarettes? Why bother when God never answers? Why bother when his tapestry included your unwanted lot?

This question concerned me because I respected Don Saulo and valued meaning and purpose, not religious beliefs. A senseless catastrophe struck my life without warning. It didn't matter what I deserved, wanted, or was true. Then what was prayer or hope? Wasn't I powerless?

Don Saulo listened with a sad, sweet grin. He added, "God doesn't give you the life you want. You get vitality from him." That probably resonated with many of the ladies around me, who believed in God and said, "If I weren't in prison right now, I'd be dead." God brought them here to spare them a worse destiny. A narrative about their situation eased their anguish. Saw that, but it didn't work.

I balked at Don Saulo. "Why would I need this?"

Always, Don Saulo gently turned things around on me. "If you pray for strength, God doesn't give you strength," he added. He lets you be strong."

I finally felt those words' truth. I believed my home, freedom, and future had been robbed from me, but Don Saulo showed me that I could still be brilliant, kind, generous, curious, creative, funny, and sane in the face of unjust agony.

Prayer invokes choice. The choice to overcome misfortune. Hold onto what matters. Choose ideals and beliefs that define you. Pain is white noise compared to that intention.

Perhaps unintentionally, Don Saulo convinced me of the tapestry. There may be no God or divine plan for our lives, but I can make my own tapestry. Life could be beautiful if I wanted. I could manifest reality through love.

Although I still didn't believe in an omnipotent creator, I realized that nihilism wasn't an option. There was no ultimate meaning to everything that happened to me or anyone else. However, that meaningless space presented a unique opportunity. I saw my misery as meaningless and significant. I wasn't alone in the tunnel awaiting the light. I had an amazing personal growth opportunity. I couldn't pretend God was watching out for me or freedom was coming. Whether I used it or not, Don Saulo's story about my misfortune being an opportunity was genuine.

I progressively accepted this new story, modifying and hemming it like a new outfit until it fit me. It helped me get through prison and shaped who I was: resilient and willing to learn from hardship.

While awaiting my appeal ruling on October 3, 2011, nearly four years after my imprisonment, I spent most of the day in Don Saulo's office playing music and conversing with the Catholic priest who had been my best friend in Capanne jail. Though my mom was crossing her fingers hard enough to shatter them, I had given up hope of a rational, truthful outcome and was accepting the fact that I would likely spend the next few decades here. I couldn't risk being shattered again like with that initial guilty judgment. Don Saulo seemed unconcerned. He said I'd aged 40 in four. He looked at me with the raw honesty he'd given me years earlier when we met. He said, "I believe you are innocent. Know you're heading home."

He disobeyed norms using a tape recorder. Since he might never hear my voice again, he wanted to videotape me singing and playing the piano. Despite my lack of faith, I played for him. I played and performed Cat Power's "Maybe Not."

We all do what we can

So we can do just one more thing

We won't have a thing

So we've got nothing to lose

We can all be free

Maybe not with words

Maybe not with a look

But with your mind

Correct, Don Saulo. When I returned to court, the verdict was "Assolta!" Acquitted! They rushed me back to the prison, where all the convicts, including the men's wing, were shouting "Libertà! Libertà!" as they banged their pots and metal plates against the bars. I didn't see Don Saulo as I hurried down the hallways to say farewell. A few minutes later, I was taken from those concrete walls and my dearest friend.

I've met vicious atheists and lovely believers, and I've realized that actions matter more than beliefs. I'm not trying to disprove God. If God inspires compassion and forgiveness like it did for Don Saulo, the world is better. That grace doesn't require God or believe in God. Kindness justifies itself.

Don Saulo taught me to treasure Jesus' wisdom, even if I'm an atheist. Turning the other cheek, the golden rule, radical nonjudgment, and acceptance of all—sinners and saints. No one deserves God's grace, but it's available to all. I view kindness that way. Kindness reserved for the virtuous, good, and kind is not kindness. I never thought I would approach my prosecutor and be friendly to him when I exited prison that day. However, I realized that true compassion and charity must be shown to everyone, even and perhaps especially to our enemies.

We can only be free then.

CHAPTER 9
Just Enough and Not at All

I roamed the room at night, unable to sleep. I heard every minute sound and potential hazard during the day. A window looked out onto the yard, where others could stretch their legs but not me. That window was always closed. I barely ate. Washing my underwear in the sink. As I sat on the foreign bed, I peered at photos of my family—they seemed remote, locked away in a time I couldn't remember, while I was stuck in this cage where I had spent years.

My Perugia prison cell is not the topic. Specifically, my childhood bedroom.

After my 2011 acquittal, my family evacuated. A local Italian politician and an ex-FBI agent helped us escape Perugia, paparazzi slamming my stepdad's car from behind, until we lost them in the night, reunited with my mom, and reached a safe house in Rome. I sat in a chair and watched my mom sleep across the room since I was too nervous to sleep. I was completely awake when the former FBI agent checked in before daybreak. "Everything okay?" he questioned.

"I can't go to sleep," I said. "I'm afraid this is a dream and I'll wake up in my cell."

"It's not a dream," he remarked.

A generous British Airways supporter upgraded me to first class for my early morning flight to Seattle. A smart precaution; journalists on the flight tried to reach me by passing notes and creeping up the 747 stairs. After everyone fell asleep, I turned on the TV. Then it hit me. Every news channel—ABC, NBC, CBS, CNN, Fox, BBC—blasted my story. I was the "famous" prisoner whose story was reported on every Italian TV station, and I knew from letters from around the world that it was international news. In my ten-by-12-foot cell, I was relatively immune to the global media bombardment. I was fighting for my freedom in court. The fact that the case was making headlines abroad didn't prepare me for channel surfing. I realised my issues were far from ended.

I emerged from bars and barbed wire into a new jail of camera lenses, flashbulbs, scary automobiles, and helicopters. Every news channel broadcast my landing at SeaTac airport, with Anderson Cooper narrating. After four years in Capanne, I was desperate for solitude and time with my family, but a throng of media crowded around a microphone, some using ladders to film my homecoming. Around fifty people had gathered at the airport to welcome me home, and I felt obligated to say something to them. I struggled to say thanks, then we jumped into three identical SUVs like a robbery movie. Helicopters circled above, ready to chase. News vans and onlookers surrounded my mom's house. We lost the paparazzi because each SUV went in a separate direction. It also prevented me from returning home. We visited my aunt and then a rental house we hoped would stay quiet.

The whole family was there to welcome my return. That night blurred. I couldn't eat and kept saying Italian unconsciously. We hid there for a few days until reporters followed my dad from his house and found us. We returned to my mom's. The house was encircled. News crews set up across the street with cameras, telephoto lenses, microphones, and satellite-dish vehicles.

Mom closed all the curtains and hasn't opened them since. While I was visiting, her neighbor said, "I remember when you first came home. I'll never forget helicopter noise." I won't either. My first few days out of prison were a tumble into a bizarre, perplexing, and unhomey environment.

My childhood bedroom was covered in flowers. After my release, my buddies opened a flower business with everything they had. The gesture was romantic, but it showed how strange that space had become. Two years of college and four years in prison had passed since I slept there. It felt more like a time capsule of me at seventeen than my own room. My stepdad's disassembled drum equipment crowded the closet. Prison mail boxes tumbled from under the bed. The patchwork quilt I sewed as a teenager, the two tall bookshelves full of novels, schoolbooks, and manga comics, the alcove with a few dozen of my stuffed animals, a poster of fairies and a clock I hand-painted in middle school, and the closet full of clothes I didn't fit and wouldn't wear were all there. I noticed the green peacoat Mom purchased me for court on my guilty judgment day. Imagine donning that horrible clothing again made me cringe.

The few remaining birds chirped in the boughs. The October leaves rustled on the trees, but the cameras outside clattered like locusts as I tried to peep through the slats. I could see the prison window.

Everything around me exacerbated my claustrophobia. Everything is supposed to be my stuff—on top, within, and behind. I vented in my room. My favorite Pokémon cards and manga collection, stuffed animals, and old clothes are going. I filled bags for Goodwill, some of which Mom hid in her closet. It was rash, but it worried me so much that what I considered "mine" didn't feel like mine. My younger self had no concept how harsh the world might be and how useless all this material was against a tide of injustice, so it felt like it belonged to the past.

I almost took down the fairy poster, but I kept marveling at its purples and greens and fairies and frogs and mushrooms. I suddenly remembered my boyhood hidden spot.

Most youngsters have areas they know or care about where magic may be feasible. My short passageway connected my house's back to my neighbor's chain-link fence. Lilacs grew along the fence. Mom didn't mow back there since it was out of the way and the ground was uneven, so the thick, flat grass stalks reached my waist and accumulated dew. My sister, Deanna, and I dared each other to go in and fetch handfuls of banana-chip-looking leaves, pretending to eat them, when it was dark and eerie with spiderwebs. Sometimes, when the sun was at the correct angle to illuminate the tunnel, spiraling motes of dust sparkled in the air, making it feel like a place where fairies lived.

I entered alone one morning when the light was perfect. The quiet rang. I wanted something like the openings of books I'd read—a closet of furs opening on a frozen wood. I wanted the fairies to see my childlike innocence and expose themselves. I walked gingerly, disturbing the grass. A burst of light through the canopy leaves!

I knew it was probably the sun. I knew I may have dreamed it. I was just old enough to know what I knew, believed, and wanted to be true. By this point, I recognized that people believed in God, and that believing in God wasn't like clustering dry beans on your desk to calculate three times three is nine. Santa Claus was fake, but my family pretended he was real for fun. I pondered if I could believe anything because I wanted to, because it made my sister happy to believe it with me, or because it made my family pleased to think I believed.

The fairy's flash of light was never mentioned. Not even Deanna, whom I confessed everything to, especially this. What I saw made me happy and curious. I felt special. However, I worried I was acting. It felt lovely to believe in something I wanted to believe in, but I knew the actual world would tear my fairy apart like tissue paper if I examined and explained it. I let that burst of light be a hidden emotion between fantasy and reality. The boundaries of my heart are a space for beliefs, imaginations, dreams, wishes, and fairies, just enough and not enough.

As I got older, I preserved the amazement and desire to believe in impossible things, even if I became a skeptic who valued rationality. Perugia, with its meandering cobblestone alleyways, pastel homes, birds, bells, and dry cypress and olive aroma, lit that spark readily. The first five weeks were amazing, not like an Instagram hashtag over a holiday sunset. That flare of light brought back childish wonder. I followed rulers, saints, and Renaissance painters. I discovered a refreshing way of life where coffee was sipped and savored at a counter, not guzzled on the go, where fresh tomatoes and cheese were enough for a meal, where no day was too busy for a siesta, and where even the most banal Italian words were spoken. When I met Raffaele, our love looked unlikely yet inevitable. The sweet, bashful, nerdy Italian lad I kiss, cook, and read with. My life had never been open.

Suddenly, those possibilities vanished. My astonishment turned terrifying strange. As if my life were on stage, the lighting technician had turned on a switch, casting spooky shadows. Prison is an exotic place where you must rethink almost everything. For years, I didn't open doors. They had keyholes instead of handles, and Agente's huge keys became handles when inserted. I was escorted from room to room, so I got used to waiting like a dog unable to operate the basic mechanism that kept me bound. The way personnel and volunteers went through the prison and unlocked doors felt like smoke. Before and after visitation with my mom, I was strip-searched. Remove your clothing, twirl, kneel, and cough.

Though terrifying at first, it became usual. Prison's oppressive drab sameness, arbitrary harshness, and casual indifference were designed to kill curiosity and hope. Trying to maintain wonder was like holding a match amid a deluge of rain.

I believed it was gone forever. I remembered it fully with this crazy fairy poster. The second wonder wave since my liberation hit me. I smelled rain and pine trees like smelling salts when I got off the airport a few days earlier, but the mainstream media couldn't catch it. The Pacific Northwest was a distant idea, a faded drawing in an old book, dusty like Capanne's land. I needed that scent to truly exist.

I met my Italian professor in the woods to hunt for chanterelle mushrooms a week after incarceration, escaping the media's attention. After years of standing on concrete, the forest floor's soft pine needle bed felt like it could lift me up. I was a moonbound astronaut.

Forest silence was healing. Everywhere else, no matter how slowly I went, everything buzzed. Hummingbirds hurried about me. I was meeting new lawyers, investigators, and supporters who had supported my family and reconnecting with loved ones I hadn't seen in years. The world pressured me to tell my experience "before it was too late." I received DVDs from all news networks covering the case. Film, book, and interview pitches rushed in via phone and letter. Why no response to my email? Besides fancy love letters, lingerie gifts, and death threats. I was known by everyone, even strangers. Some came to me in the grocery store, crying with excitement. I'm delighted you returned. Sometimes they looked at me from across the street with black eyes.

The circus ended after a few weeks, but I was still followed and photographed when I went to the shop or walked the dogs. Mom advised me to move carefully, but I wanted my own room. For four years in prison, my friend Madison and I wrote letters about obtaining an apartment together when I returned. We found a little two-bedroom apartment in International District, Seattle. My family recommended against it. "It's not safe," they said. No security in the building." It was true. An unethical paparazzo or crazed killer may easily enter the building and walk to our unit. What I didn't want to hear after losing so much time was that I had to wait longer. No. I could no longer wait to live.

In reverse, I did. I acted quickly. The wonder of moving into that modest flat made me dizzy. The keys were barely noticeable, yet they were mine and felt heavy and large in my hand, like they could open a metropolis. I had nearly forgotten what it felt like to hold a key and control a door, even if it led to a little kitchen. No living area, just the kitchen, my room (smaller than my prison cell), Madison's room, and the bathroom. A turn-of-the-century hotel room became a fourth-floor walkup. We spent $788 a month for that little freedom.

New neighborhood streets made me feel like the new girl on the cellblock, like everyone was judging me. Just like the new girl on the cellblock, I kept my head down and looked away. Every time I went out alone in public, my sensation of impending peril crept up my neck. I'd see the lumbering silhouette of an inmate I knew out of the corner of my eye and jump, only to realize it was a stranger walking by. I would cross the street anyway.

I felt more vulnerable than at my mom's house, but rushing in was worth it. In the middle of metropolitan life, most people didn't recognize me. Incredible meal. In high school, I bought manga comics at Uwajimaya, a culinary paradise. I was queen and the fruit aisle was my kingdom for a few glorious minutes each day. The Goodwill was walking distance, so I regularly swapped out court and prison clothes for bright, joyful attire. Our apartment was in Pioneer Square, Seattle's oldest area with art galleries, boutiques, and chic restaurants. One of my favorite independent bookstores, Arundel Books, sold secondhand and rare books there. I felt like Aladdin in the treasure hoard as I entered. I sniffed the books, stroked their spines, and bought as many as I could carry.

Again alone, anxious and bewildered, my curiosity was piqued. Magic returned, things I never dreamed were conceivable, and who knew what strange surprise was around the next corner? As time went on, I felt like I was experiencing someone else's dream that I couldn't wake up from.

CHAPTER 10
Self-Help

You'd think I'd be a therapy junkie after all I'd been through. But you're mistaken.

Before my acquittal, Mom believed I would need lots of treatment. She continually told me that therapy would help me heal after years in prison when I got home. I said, "Or, I'm fine."

"That's impossible," she said.

"I'm FINE," I said, sounding fine.

Talking to a stranger who didn't know my story was unsettling. Therapy was forced on me in prison. Psychiatrists occasionally came to "help" convicts, but I thought they prescribed drugs. Antidepressants are prescribed for depression. After claiming withdrawal, you obtain methadone. Their "help" was evident in the medicated slumber of cellmates who had doped themselves blank to get through the day, week, or years. I avoided them.

Agente forced me into the psychiatrist's office after I shaved off all my hair after being convicted.

"You wanted to see me."

"I did not want to see you."

Okay, they brought you to visit me. How can I help?

"Nothing. You can't help me."

"You're fine?"

I'm fine."

«I saw you trimmed your hair»

"I can cut my hair."

"I don't think you're fine."

It meant what? The women around me used olive oil to condition, comb, and braid their hair. Sometime, I did. I kept my long hair as a connection to the outside world. After prison, I'd want my long, lovely hair.

After my conviction, my hair felt like disgusting vanity. Not going home. My prisoner status. Why the hell did I need lovely hair?

Prosecutors and media called me a seductress. Cutting my hair off was a massive middle finger to those charges and a severe reality check.

"You can't help me," I told the psychiatrist. "May I leave?"

I thought of that exchange whenever Mom mentioned therapy. I tried to ignore it, but Mom is stubborn. I was begged to visit a trauma specialist at the University of Washington. I agreed to show her I didn't need it.

Students frequented the Ave, a strip of clubs and eateries near college, where the office was located. At five p.m. on a frigid winter day, it was dark. Knocked his office door. I arrived to see him behind his desk after he contacted me. It looked like a professor's office stock shot. Books, framed degrees, desk photographs, plant. He appeared unremarkable in his jacket, glasses, and soft "trauma specialist" demeanor. He hid in his dark hair. I said I didn't know what to say. "That's okay," he said. "Just sit." My seat was awkward. He asked, "So, how are you doing?"

Then my chest fell. That was intended to be a simple inquiry, but it felt impossible to respond.

Not being okay wasn't an option. I needed to be okay to endure prison. Anything else was weakness that might be exploited. Freedom felt the same. Paradoxically, I thought that if I was ever not fine, it was in a jail, and now that I was out, I should have been fine. I deserved to be okay after surviving so long. I desperately wanted that.

I was sobbing in front of this stranger. With each gulp, my thinking alternated between being angry at myself for proving Mom correct and angry at Mom because I had been holding it together until she forced me into this room. Before Italy, I was outgoing and friendly, watching people. I sometimes visited the Pike Place Market on my way home from high school and wandered its convoluted corridors to escape into a world of busy strangers. I stopped talking to strangers. Not trusting people. I figured everyone wanted to exploit me. Even if this therapist had good intentions, he had no idea what I was going through. No one did. People couldn't help me; they made things worse. They only confirmed that I belonged nowhere.

I gasped, "Sorry. Cannot do it. I must leave." Professor had no time to say goodbye. I left.

Maybe I wasn't okay. I tried therapy again later at Mom's suggestion. To avoid being traced, I paid a woman $300 an hour in cash. I feared being betrayed and sold to tabloids. I talked for hours, hoping for a breakthrough. I thought this worked for others, but not me. Just another way I didn't belong. I left after two months.

Madison then got me to attend a Vipassana silence retreat. Meditation, silence, tranquility, and healing were perfect for me. The administrator contacted beforehand to ask about my meditation history. "This is intense," she said. "Ten days without talking, hours of meditation." I told her I spent four years in prison. I thought I could do this if I could do that.

Stepdad dropped me off at the retreat facility. It was just a few buildings in a field. I didn't find it quiet or beautiful.

The first morning was unpleasant. They showed a two-hour film of a guru explaining meditation and metaphysical nonsense. I had no idea I had signed up for ten days of indoctrination. We then walked in the field for an hour of meditation. The prison yard was the last time I had to walk in a loop repeatedly. I attempted to dismiss that thinking. We had lentils in the cafeteria for lunch and were told not to converse or make eye contact. I appreciated it because I didn't want to be identified, but that was also how I'd behaved in prison—keeping my head down, avoiding eye contact, and attempting to blend in to avoid being seen.

They made us meditate for three hours in our cramped dorm rooms. After 30 minutes, claustrophobia overcame me. I returned to the field and tried walking meditation, but a supervisor advised me to go back to my room. Despite my explanation, they persisted. Feeling chastened, I returned. Minutes later, terror struck. I sobbed out of the room and was taken to the lead instructor's office.

I told her I couldn't do it, that too much was like prison, and I had to leave. She kept me there for 30 minutes to see if I needed to leave or simply calm down. "I must be able to go," I said. I really can't do this in your office."

I died in a day. I grabbed my things and contacted Mom to pick me up that afternoon. The ride home was agonizingly quiet. Again, I felt like I'd shown them I was a mess. I felt incoherent rage again: They don't know what I've been through or what I need, and I was great until someone pushed me into this.

I recognized my mental health treatment endeavors failed because I was doing them for others—my mom, my friend—not myself. Despite avoiding therapy and meditation, I processed my trauma. I often walked or biked alone, contemplating. Many hours. I walked the library stacks. From the International District to UW, I would walk five miles. I'd lazily browse Goodwill's vast store. I was observing everything, big and little, as if they were equal. I felt lost and insignificant like a ghost. Haunted. For a while, it helped. You might be surprised how little I talked about my trauma. I hadn't realized that it could help others and that finding purpose in misery was uniquely soothing.

Going up for myself in prison wouldn't have worked. It would have been violent. I endured a lot of crap and shrank. I believed independence would return me to my size, but it didn't. I still felt little as the world watched me for anything it could use to denigrate me.

When I returned to Mom's house, I saw a photo of myself as a teenager, wearing my soccer gear and smiling with a naïve trust in the world. The girl in the photo was fine. Personally, no.

CHAPTER 11
Public Property

In early 2012, a few months after my release from prison, someone first sat me down and explained what a "public figure" was. Now that I had grimaced through all the press corps' DVDs, I was beginning to understand Foxy Knoxy's various faces and how he stood in my way to reintegration into free society. My media dissection and distortion seemed criminal. I met with two lawyers in Seattle and was told to watch the made-for-TV Lifetime film Amanda Knox: Murder on Trial in Italy, where Hayden Panettiere played me, and list every fact the producers got wrong. I sued the film to delete a dream scenario where Amanda murders Meredith while I was in prison appealing my sentence. Beyond that, libel may be possible.

As I played the DVD they gave me, I tried to fall into the same state of numbness I had in the courtroom, where I spent hundreds of hours silently listening to people discuss theories, gruesome facts, and insignificant details to determine if I was a monster.

The film had several big and small mistakes. Paused every few seconds to write them down. My Seattle coffee shop was a small mom-and-pop with a nice wine selection, but they portrayed it as Starbucks. My coworker called me "Foxy Knoxy," but no one in college called me that childhood soccer moniker. Dressed around her cleavage, Hayden Panettiere portrayed me as a drug dealer connoisseur. Television cameras caught her smiling and waving.

This and other tabloid-style tidbits set my heart racing. I had to take breaks to stay cool, but I returned to my lawyers with a huge list and the disturbing understanding that most people thought this had happened. Most people saw me as this.

I figured we could sue Lifetime. In addition to minor mistakes, the film contained important factual errors, such as having Raffaele phone the police to report the break-in after they arrived, making him look like a liar trying to cover something up. In the movie, investigators mistakenly interrogated me as a suspect when I was merely a witness and refused a lawyer. They didn't show when a detective beat me in the back of the head or when I recanted my coerced remarks incriminating Patrick Lumumba.

My lawyers agreed these were substantial factual errors. But there was an issue. Factual inaccuracies didn't prove libel. A public figure, I had to prove the filmmakers deliberately distorted these facts with malice. We would need to subpoena their documents, which could take months and yield nothing, and "Foxy Knoxy" would make headlines again.

I objected. Was this fair? I didn't want to be "the girl accused of murder." But I knew my objections were weak. I had lost this battle many times. Lifetime wasn't the worst by far. It bothered me that, again, others were determining who I was, the truth didn't matter, and I couldn't do anything about it.

Public figures have no expiration date. There's no clear line between a public figure's public and private lives. As a public celebrity, I had no legal remedy when cameras followed me to a waltz lesson and tabloids told a deceptive story that I might as well have been dancing on Meredith's grave. Without outright lying or malevolent intent, I had to let this erroneous and lurid content circulate through the media ecosystem. One tabloid would print such a story, another would pick it up, and another, until more reputable outlets like NBC saw the click-and-cash opportunity and put out a more sanitized version that retained the disparaging frame of the original article, changing through social media's distorted gossip network.

Can you believe her Halloween costume? She sings karaoke? Which singer will never sing karaoke again? Meredith. Defending myself only led to charges that I was a narcissist seeking attention, a liar, and a killer.

Many don't grasp how this feels. Often, my family did not. During my trial, I learnt that my family would do everything for me. They remained devoted even when my hatred spilled over into them: "Foxy Knoxy, the girl who had to compete with her own mother for men"; "Foxy Knoxy's sisters posing happily for 'macabre' photos at the house where Meredith Kercher died." They put their mental health, relationships, and finances on hold to save Amanda. Capanne gave me six hours of visitation a month and made sure someone was there for me for four years. They never missed those valuable hours.

When I was released, acquitted, and returned home, they wanted to return to their old lives, and I did too. They deserved it. After the nightmare, people could prioritize themselves, resume hobbies and passions, and return to their old behaviors. But I couldn't. Foxy Knoxy lived in the media.

One-way mirrors disguised men in white coats with clipboards in a lab that recreated freedom. Imagine drinking coffee in a café. Your companion returns from the bathroom and says a man in the corner is taking your photo with his phone. He writes about you in his notebook: what you wear, how you look, what you think, whether you enjoy harsh sex or hard drugs. Do you act like he's gone? Living your life? Should you leave? Report it to the police? I was powerless to stop people from observing and guessing about me everywhere I went and did.

Whether it's a newspaper across the ocean or a café stalker, our ears burn when someone talks about us. I wish I could claim I succeeded despite this constant attention, but, no. That judgmental lens made me uneasy, wary, and withdrawn, or suggestible and eager to please. If I had been able to immerse myself in normal life, my refusal of therapy and insistence on being fine may have worked. Instead, I was in a twisted universe that made it nearly impossible to understand and integrate my life's struggles and traumas.

But that was my issue. I mistakenly believed a story about me written by others. I was trying to reform myself in the story, but I was still in a bad situation. I felt like the villain in someone else's story, not the author. I immediately realized that responding to lies was futile. But I couldn't ignore the last four years. I realized I couldn't ignore how my experience had altered me. For better or worse, I had to experience being wrongfully accused in my life and career, like in Capanne. That encounter needed processing. But unlike in Capanne, where I had to accept my fate and make the best of it, now I felt like I had a nebulous opportunity, a duty, to intervene on my behalf and change my fate. It can take years, decades, or my whole life, but I tried.

I also owed my family, lawyers, and the numerous individuals who had volunteered to save me. To digest my trauma and repay my family, writing a memoir was the greatest way to make them whole again. Opening myself to the world. It meant growing as big as possible and taking up as much space as possible. I knew I would be a bigger target as I grew.

CHAPTER 12
Defensive Maneuvers

For years, I felt small and voiceless as strangers discussed who I was, what I did, and what I deserved. I believed publishing a memoir would finally let me speak up and help me find my place in this new world.

I found writing Waiting to Be Heard harder and more cathartic than expected. I got angry remembering little details of Capanne—how the warden had balked at my dismay after seeing Meredith's autopsy images, how other convicts had tormented me and gossiped behind my back—and had to get up from my computer and go around my block. My anger had been suppressed for years. Even though I was exhausted at the end of the day, recalling those events helped me understand them.

I realized this could be a turning point toward the end of the book. I might finally be seen for who I was and move on from this tragedy. If I wanted anyone to read it, I had to promote it, which would put me in the sensational and judgmental limelight I'd been avoiding since I got home.

I had never given an interview, and I hoped that when I did, my distrust would turn into understanding. On March 26, 2013, Italy's Court of Cassation overturned my acquittal and ordered a retrial just over a month before the memoir's publication.

The panic I felt was beyond shock. What did that mean? For months, I knew that the Court of Cassation, Italy's Supreme Court, would have to uphold my acquittal, and my lawyers told me that my prosecutor, Dr. Giuliano Mignini, was furious and that the state would appeal. But I thought this was largely formal. I thought my innocence was proven when the appeals court recruited two independent specialists to refute the DNA evidence on the murder weapon, my lone link to the crime. They delivered their results to a raucous court. Independent specialists shattered Dr. Mignini's case. I could not have participated in a terrible death orgy and avoided detection. How could you argue with that? I thought it was the end of this drama, so I wasn't ready to be in serious danger again. However, I was on trial again for the same crime.

Despite my memoir's impending publication, I began discussing extradition treaties and in absentia defense with my counsel. It felt like my voice and views needed to be heard more than ever. Of course, I wanted the book to succeed. I was contractually required to promote it. Since I returned home, every journalist sought me. At trial again, there would be no softball, sympathetic interviews. Anyone I spoke to would rather interrogate Foxy Knoxy, on trial for murder again, than Amanda Knox, who had served four years for a crime she didn't commit. Even professional journalists who wanted to correct misconceptions saw me as a valuable "get." Was a commodity.

My lawyers chose Matt Lauer at NBC, Diane Sawyer at ABC, and Oprah Winfrey. I met Matt Lauer in NYC. He was nice, but I was tired of middle-aged males grilling me, so I preferred a woman. I called Oprah, who was kind and intelligent. I could tell she understood. My lawyers knew she was my choice, but there was a catch. I would interview Oprah following her conversation with Lance Armstrong. That didn't seem well to my lawyers. They advised me to choose ABC's Diane Sawyer.

I made this decision on a phone call with my team in the few minutes between courses while strolling through the UW quad under the cherry blossoms, keeping my head down to avoid recognition. ABC had covered my case well, and Nikki Battiste, a journalist who had grown close to my family during my imprisonment, would create the hour-long special. I hadn't spoken to Diane Sawyer. I still regret not choosing Oprah.

ABC hired a loft in lower Manhattan for filming and put me up at the Waldorf Astoria in a huge room—I was still used to my cell and modest flat back home. I was unprepared for this crucial first interview. Tina, my book publicist, purchased me an outfit from J.Crew, far from Goodwill, my favorite store. My lawyers advised me to repeat my book's title throughout the interview. They showed me a video of Hillary Clinton using Hard Choices every other sentence.

"Diane is going to ask you some tough questions," they added, "but you've answered them many times. Just stay calm."

Diane was kind yet distant. She didn't seem warm. In that professional atmosphere, she was performing her job, therefore I should answer her questions. That mentality made me accept that I was on trial again and would have to answer, "Did you kill Meredith Kercher?" for the millionth time. When I said "No," the world would look for duplicity in my face. Asking the question implied ambiguity, making me a figure to doubt. Diane only wanted to doubt my innocence. She didn't care about me and asked whether I liked my fame.

Diane departed after two hours of the seven-hour interview, but another producer finished the rest. When the interview aired, they trimmed my seven hours to 10 minutes and filled the remainder with Diane's case presentation.

My face, trauma, and reputation played on prime-time television and mega screens in Times Square. My innocence was debated in every rag in the checkout line, and countless tweets and posts, making me feel uncomfortably large, so big, so public, as if every street person was in the jury box.

A week later, I spent days addressing the same questions from print and radio journalists at my publisher's headquarters. Did you murder Meredith Kercher? No. How do you feel about retrial? Devastated. They hammered me about Patrick Lumumba in a live radio interview with an Australian broadcaster. Why wrongfully accuse an innocent man? I didn't know how to describe police pressure, how they had systematically broken me down over fifty-three hours of questioning, threatened, assaulted, and gaslit me until I signed an unintelligible statement. I called the interrogation the scariest thing ever, but the interrogator persisted. Tina snatched the phone and hung up as I stared helpless.

Chris Cuomo was interviewed last-minute. Chris entered CNN's makeup room and said, "I'm going to ask you some tough questions, but just so you know, I'm only doing it so you can answer them." Many will seem silly, but they're the questions people are asking, and I want to offer you a chance to address them."

We sat on a raised dais with dramatic lighting and enormous screens behind me showing crime scene and trial footage. He pushed me through the interview, like he wanted me to respond quickly to the preposterous charges. "What about this mop I keep hearing about?" He meant the mop I brought from home to Raffaele's the morning Meredith's death was found. The task was to mop up leaking sink water in Raffaele's kitchen, but Dr. Giuliano Mignini initially suspected I had cleaned up the crime scene. Although the mop had no blood or DNA, the crime scene showed no indications of cleaning. Chris knew and admitted it. We asked another irrelevant but harmful question. Were you into deviant sex? Maybe insensitive, but we must get to the truth. This raises doubt."

Chris Cuomo still thinks he helped me. He repeated it on Twitter. He didn't realize that his queries were casting doubt on my character.

After the interview, he asked, "What would you say to those who continue to doubt your innocence?"

"Speculation convicts me," I responded, "but evidence acquits me."

Tina, my publicist, and lawyers were thrilled! Who told you to say that? "I just thought of it," I added, receiving high fives.

The cutting room floor got that line. Despite my best efforts in these interviews, my innocence was irrelevant. This was changed and molded to suit the journalist and network, who released the version with the most clicks. CNN showed viewers desperation. Cuomo asked, "Five years from today, what do you want in your life?"

"I hope to be definitively found innocent," I said. "I don't know how long I can last. I can't defend myself forever. I cannot imagine defending myself against murder charges for the rest of my life."

Cuomo concluded the program by saying, "We may never know exactly what happened in the villa on the night of November first, 2007," and that "Amanda Knox's behavior and her incriminating words remain around her neck, like a noose."

I was panicked in my hotel after this lengthy interview week. I tried to relax with a bath, but it failed. I was fatigued and my breathing raced by bedtime. My body reflected my inability to control my life. Interrogations continued endlessly. Would I always have to defend myself against ridiculous accusations? Why was I alive? Why was I alive? Why?

I knew my lawyers, publicist, and advocates would have jumped in front of a bus for me. They forced me into this media nightmare. That's how things went. Their environment had rules. No one considered, Actually, these rules will produce additional trauma.

The frame was problematic. Like Dr. Giuliano Mignini, everyone looked to me for answers. They questioned me about a crime scene I'd never seen. Rudy Guede, Meredith's killer, should have been asked the same questions. If I had known then what I know now, I would have responded, "Look, if you're here to ask me about Meredith's murder, I know just as much. No special replies for you. I can describe what it feels like to be going about my business and then being arrested for something I didn't commit. "I can talk your head off about that!"

Without that words, I gasped for air. My test answers were graded, even though I didn't know them. The test was based on my guilt and deserving judgment. When did you quit hitting your wife? I was locked in my life, not a cell.

Tired from crying and heaving, I passed asleep that night. My panic came from a growing sense that this would never change. My book wasn't important. Not a turning point. My noose would never be cut by anything I did or said.

CHAPTER 13
Just Ignore It

Not even I faced the first death threat. For my mom. Within weeks of arriving in Capanne, I was a magnet for hostility. As I read the letter in my cell, this stranger said he knew where my mother was in Perugia and would kill her to punish me. I informed Agente immediately. You must act! My mom needs security!"

"Just ignore it," she urged.

Next threat, then next. After four years in prison, I stopped counting death threats. It became part of my surreal reality. My family and friends' flat on Perugia's outskirts was not being stalked. Major physical dangers to my well-being occurred within Capanne's walls, including Vice Commandante Argirò, male agents, and unruly inmates. I naively believed my acquittal would end the threats.

However, the threats and harassment remained while I tried to rebuild a regular life at home, and they only increased after my second trial. They arrived at my mom's house in the mail and in the comments on my site where I posted official statements as the case changed. Among supportive letters, some wished me dead and described how it would happen. After my memoir and prime-time interrogations, this grew worse. The same warped mind kept threatening me, pursuing their murderous fantasies. One determined death-wisher wrote that he would arrive in an unmarked van and take me in broad daylight because he didn't care if he was caught. I would be taken somewhere no one could hear me scream and Meredith's name carved into my body. He would electrocute me with a car battery, enjoying my pain. He tortured me till I pleaded for mercy and tried to trade sex, like a slut. He refused. Only when I pleaded for death did he kill me.

I asked retired FBI Special Agent Steve Moore for help. He planned and executed my thrilling escape from Italy. Now he connected me to the local FBI field office. They found the man who sent me those graphic threats. They invited the Royal Canadian Mounties to see him because he was Canadian. I imagined Dudley Do-Right riding to his door. I learnt from the FBI that he was an elderly security guard. His wife seemed as surprised as I was that he sent those messages. The Mounties relayed an FBI warning, but that was all they could do. Nothing could be done unless he bought an airline ticket to Seattle to carry out his threats.

Strangely, the darkest items wounded me least. One may easily recognize that Canadian man as mentally ill and that I was his victim. But folks like him were rare compared to the casual vitriol on social media directed at me. Both vigilante groups were righteous and gave me what I deserved.

All my friends and relatives used social media. Even Oma used Facebook. I kept my Facebook and Instagram accounts private for close friends and family because I knew what would happen if I entered that world. That didn't stop the harsh comments when my case made headlines or someone produced another YouTube video slandering my handwriting, hand gestures, or facial tics.

Public posts usually backfired for me. Before the retrial, I shared a photo of myself holding a handwritten sign reading "Siamo Innocenti"—We Are Innocent. Italians replied by sharing duplicate photos of themselves holding "Perugia Vi Odia" placards or photoshopping my message to say "Cercasi Coinquilina"—Roommate Wanted.

All this showed me how destructive social media was before society accepted it.

Online anonymity, instant interaction over great distances, cultural echo chambers, and rampant misinformation made combating abuse and antisocial conduct difficult. Targeted harassment has been easy to pass through algorithmic abuse controls on platforms that filter terms to minimize online hate. I often get messages like, "We know you did it," and "How do you sleep at night?" Or just "Meredith." I received photos of Meredith and my house from a troll. That's a major harassment blow. The computer sees a house, but I and the troll know what it represents—a crime scene.

Though my instance is extreme, I know this happens at a lower volume worldwide. In addition to death threats, I receive communications from girls and young women who describe being denigrated and harassed online and in social circles. I remember how my high school boys openly speculated about me and the other girls—"Is she a S? No, maybe she's T? I think she's F." We were appalled to learn they were discussing our pubic hair—shaved, trimmed, or "forest." If kids can objectify and degrade one other in front of teachers, social media makes it easier. Specific, targeted harassment hurts most. I had an awkward menstruation episode in algebra. When that happens to a student nowadays, a spiteful classmate might easily get through social media abuse filters with a targeted word like "seat stainer."

We may debate incentives, rules, algorithms, and AI to reduce online hate, bullying, and harassment. But personally, what do you think of someone who hates you, wants you dead, or wants your mother dead because she raised you?

First, I didn't know how to react. It didn't help that my struggle was distinct in degree, not kind, from all women's uphill battle to have a voice online. I wasn't happy with most of my well-wishers' counsel. Men frequently said, "If you can't take the heat, get out of the kitchen." Women said, "The block button is your best friend." After Agente told me about the first death threat in prison, I attempted to ignore it for a long time but failed. A death threat or harsh comment online would destroy my day.

It helped to keep reminding myself that none of these folks despised me. My image was loathed. So I was lucky. I was eventually able to separate myself from the object of my hate because it was so strong, pervasive, irrational, and founded on so many lies. I stopped taking things personally. Most of the time. Although the object they loathed looked like me, shared my name, and would affect my life in the future, I was not disliked.

This insight has two sides. It means that when people applaud me—and they do—it's not always about me. This is about my idea again. The absence of overlap between me and that avatar is extreme, especially negative. The Foxy Knoxy criticisms have little to do with me, and while I like to think the praise matches who I am, the more essential lesson is that I am not "Amanda Knox," the public figure.

This gap between how you see yourself and how others see you is an opportunity to reflect, reassess, and better define yourself. It can also help you understand others' self-stories, since they often utilize you as a prop. As black goes with white, on with off, we naturally define ourselves in opposition to others. We stay safe in the good guys' circle by labeling others the bad people. It doesn't feel that way. We judge others because we compare ourselves to them, even though it feels like we're judging them.

This understanding helped me comprehend why my arrest and conviction authority never admitted fault, even trying me for the same crime twice. Acknowledging their failures would damage their self-stories as competent justice providers, compelling them to accept a new identity as harm-makers.

In time, I learned to see each new barb of hate, each threat, as a reminder of who I was and who I wanted to be: a person who would try her damndest not to get sucked into false beliefs and to always be on guard against that righteous feeling, that vigilante impulse, because it's so easy to harm others while believing ourselves to be champions for justice. I don't like vengeful thinking, but I've learned to value becoming my best self.

CHAPTER 14
The Bunker

As hard as it was to acclimate to the surreal world of freedom and try to start again, accepting that I would always be judged, scrutinized, and hated were psychological issues. I figured I would figure things out. Italy didn't abandon me.

The second trial, which began September 30, 2013, was even absurder. The forensic evidence that acquitted me was undisputed. There was no fake DNA to prove my guilt. Inspired by Dr. Giuliano Mignini, my new prosecutor used indirect witness testimonies and behavioral evidence to present me as a drugged, sexually deviant femme fatale again. The trial seemed more preoccupied with my guilt or innocence than with the murder itself. Would an innocent kiss her boyfriend outside the crime scene? Would she smear an innocent man? Could this be the behavior of someone who was clearly involved in the crime, even if we can't determine what? "How can you separate the slander from the murder?" asked Dr. Mignini in an interview.

I'd heard this argument before. It was a favorite line of argument for online trolls outraged by my legal victory. It was also the most popular answer to the nagging why question: Why was I wrongfully accused? Many who believed in my innocence thought I did it. Despite being innocent, I acted guilty. I had a unique problem.

Naturally, being blamed for my unjust conviction and evaluated in the worst light made me worried, but the case was so ambiguous and thin. I was hopeful. Raffaele and I were convicted again on January 30, 2014. Sentence was increased from 26 to 28.5 years.

My attorneys and I had one of the most heated, screaming phone calls ever. "How is this possible?" My screech. "How could they convict me without evidence?"

Rome-based attorney Carlo Dalla Vedova was like my dad in Italian. He was beautiful, personable, straight-shooting, dignified, professional, warm, and a family man. One of my fondest recollections from his visit to Capanne was when he winked at me to eat gelato as a balanced dinner. His voice sounded strained and muffled. "Not over. We can yet appeal to the Cassation Court."

The Court of Cassation overturned my acquittal?

It didn't feel real because this trial was over five thousand miles away and without my participation. I watched local news updates. As if hearing shooting on TV and then seeing myself bleeding from the abdomen. I bitterly wondered if the Perugia police were rejoicing, high-fiving like they did after forcing me to sign false statements. I wondered if my prosecutor, Dr. Giuliano Mignini, felt vindicated like I did when I left Capanne.

Raffaele and I were not instantly imprisoned because I had one more chance to appeal to Italy's highest court. However, we were convicted murderers again and in limbo.

Since I could only wait, I attempted to carry on as usual, but extradition loomed large in my mind. My concern about cameras and stranger-danger increased as an axe felt constantly over my neck. Though not imprisoned, I was not free. I could not grow any roots. I had a deadline for any relationships or careers I started. I felt my life had been sidetracked for four years and was now getting to where I should have been at twenty-four. Now catching up was pointless. I had to plan for disaster. I restarted UW classes, but would I graduate? I wasn't up to such queries. My lawyers suggested contacting famous DNA scientists and fake confessions experts to challenge my conviction. I was lucky then too. Raffaele had been touring the world since our 2011 acquittal, looking for a place to settle outside Italy. A buddy half-joked about marrying him to help him become a U.S. citizen. Several times, I thought it wasn't his fault his country had turned against him. But it may not help. The U.S. government and an ocean separated me from the nation trying to send me back to prison, but if I lost my appeal, I would be sent back. I was just one American, and the US and Italy had long-standing economic, political, and military relations. My lawyers said the U.S. would not use political power to keep me out of prison if my appeal failed. It was important to follow Italy's law, even if it was defective, to retain diplomatic relations.

I would likely go to prison if convicted again. It might not have to be in Italy. My book deal lawyers in America offered to represent me pro bono in an extradition case. We planned how I would turn myself in and petition the U.S. authorities to spend my time in an American prison so my family could see me without an international flight.

While I faced this terrible reality, my family considered a riskier option. At supper, someone would imply. Someone we know knows someone. They have basements."

"What are you talking about?"

Very well-stocked. Enough for a brief visit. Boats cross into Canada from there. You'd go far north."

"Who are they?" I requested.

Names were never mentioned. I doubt they knew. Only "Supporters" were mentioned. Even though it was illegal, people helped. The answer was "No one you know," when I asked who would accompany me to chilly Canada. I would have to disappear to do this. A pencil was my most advanced carry-on.

I still don't know how serious those plans were. However, I understand why my family made them. I would be lying if I said I didn't contemplate running. My lying is bad. That partly turned me off this course. Running wasn't a stain on my character. I didn't owe Italy my life because they wouldn't acknowledge that Meredith Kercher's killer was in custody. Why did Rudy Guede not matter? His thirty-year rape and murder conspiracy sentence was reduced to sixteen years on appeal. The insaneness of pursuing me again while decreasing his sentence made me consider running more seriously. Negotiating with unfair parties is pointless.

As I imagined that life—taking on a false identity, living alone in a bunker or basement hundreds of miles from anyone I knew, dying my hair, maybe working the register at an antique store in Yellowknife on the northern shore of the Great Slave Lake, falling in love with a quiet man despite myself, only to leave him in the middle of the night for fear that he'd finally recognized me or that the truth would erupt from me spontaneously—I couldn'

What I imagined was suicide. In prison, I considered drinking bleach, ingesting glass, a garbage bag, and butane burner. I refused because I couldn't do that to my family or myself—where prison was the last thing I'd see in life. Faced with possible extradition, I considered going out on my own terms and maintaining my position to avoid prison. Entertaining the idea became routine. Madison and I discussed it while browsing Goodwill outfits. "I've thought about it," I continued, "and I think I've decided. I'd rather die here than there." She tried to encourage me to endure another appeal or guilty verdict. "I'll help you," she said. I'll get you what you need, but not now. Only if you have no option and return there."

I persevered through those awful periods because I knew that killing myself would have been a lie, even though I truly considered it. It would betray everything I'd worked for, the self I had been in Capanne, bound and aching for freedom, and the self I would become if I stayed, wherever she went.

Murder convictions had imprisoned me in my name. Running from that would let them win. I wasn't alone. People who believed I was a killer tried to get my mother fired from her primary school. If I quit, I'd never cleanse her name either. Escape from prison wasn't enough. I have to take it fighting for the truth in and out of court. I had lost track of Amanda Knox after two years in the unsteady realm of freedom. In actuality, I wasn't strong enough to defend myself throughout this seemingly endless trek. I changed identities for a while.

Normal people worked. I needed work. I realize that sounds like reading a new novel as your plane crashes, but I could be acquitted, and I had bills and days to fill. I sold my memoir for a lot, but after taxes, agent fees, and paying off my legal and family debts from 2007, most of it was gone, and I still had an appeals trial. I didn't want my family to get into further debt if I was extradited.

I agreed to work the register when the owner of the antiquarian bookstore I frequented asked me. I was already there many days a week browsing the unique variety of rare and first editions, breathing in book smell—my preferred aromatherapy. The business was underground in Pioneer Square, Seattle's oldest neighborhood. It was private, had little foot traffic—most of their books were sold online, I learned—and was great for me. My last job before Italy was a University District barista. Face-to-face encounters all day. Now I wouldn't apply for such a position. I doubt many employers wanted Amanda Knox's baggage. I knew Raffaele had problems obtaining work in Italy for that reason. Of obviously, hiring me would bring bad PR, but the stalkers, haters, and death threats raised liability concerns.

Phil, the bookstore owner, didn't care. He said I could work on shipping in the back room while he took over the counter if someone came in searching for me, which happened.

The job gave me routine, which I like. The only negatives were that it paid minimum wage, which didn't cover my monthly expenditures, and it wasn't a career start. That wouldn't matter if I was sent back to prison, but I figured I could do more than stand at a counter for the rest of my life. I didn't know what I wanted, but it came from unexpected places.

Patrick, an editor with the West Seattle Herald, which had covered my neighborhood for a century since 1923, contacted me on Facebook. "I would love for you to write for the paper," he responded. I was skeptical instantly. Naturally, he wanted me to write for the local paper. I was warned by my attorneys about such well-wishers. He didn't care if I could write. He wanted my byline to notice. I would not humiliate myself for my local newspaper.

"I read your memoir," he said. You can write! We want to let you write more. You could cover arts for us. You can even adopt a pseudonym."

Despite my reluctance to change my name—it wasn't the issue—this offer intrigued me. He didn't want to use my worst experience to sell his newspaper? Leaving Phil from the bookshop aside, I felt that was all any random stranger cared about me. Paradoxically, his offer to write under a pseudonym made me feel respected for who I was, not what my name represented.

This Herald opportunity allowed me to be creative regularly under low pressure. It improved my writing. The salary was low, but it would augment my bookshop income and launch a literary career I thought was impossible. Even though my memoir was a New York Times bestseller, I realized it wasn't because of the writing but because of people's interest in the case and myself. It didn't feel like the beginning. My entire adult life was judged by the murder charge. This position would let me create work that would be appraised on its own merits. I gladly agreed.

My thoughts went blank when I thought about my pseudonym. I wanted it to sound like a real person's name and have meaning. Because Emile was gender neutral and a character in Oma's favorite childhood tale, I selected it. My pantry had a can of Del Monte peas at eye level, so I chose Monte. Monte meant mountain in Italian, the symbolic mountain I had yet to climb. Using this alias, I would start. It was Emile Monte.

Accepted it immediately. No office visit required. I emailed my bosses. I could work in my apartment. I reviewed a local performance in a darkened venue for the press. When I interviewed local artists and authors in person, I always presented myself as Emile. My interviewers didn't say if they recognized me. Maintaining professionalism, I avoided eye contact. I was shy and withdrawn, but I tried to listen and treat people as I would have been handled in interviews.

Local circulation was low for the Herald. I reviewed high school plays and independent theater company shows for a small audience. However, that was exactly what I needed after years in the global limelight. This employment seemed like charity, like my bookshop job. It wasn't necessary for the West Seattle Herald editor to contact me or seek my pseudonymous opinion. He wanted to let me try normalcy. That was impossible for Amanda Knox. This was for Emile Monte.

Not that I've felt above criticism. Truthful judgment pleases me. If you avoid criticism, you won't improve. Being criticized for something you could have done better is a gift.

My connection with criticism was abusive. They chastised me for actions I never did and attributes I never had. Every action I took was evaluated negatively. My life was so full with judgment and criticism that, even though I tried to reject it, I couldn't stop internalizing some of it, especially the bits I didn't understand. What occurred to me in the interrogation room? What changed my personality after four years of exclusion? I urgently wanted to be judged for who I was and what I did. But even I wasn't sure how much guilt was on me and how much on the world.

Our egos are naturally linked to our achievements and disappointments. When we win, we feel great; when we lose, we feel bad. When you fail hard, repeatedly, or publicly, your self-image suffers. When that happens, you're not assessing your own behavior, but the stupid, failure, coward, or asshole you think would make that mistake. I remember Emile Monte, that faceless man, and judge my blunders on their own merits when I tend to link them to my identity. I attempt to prevent repeating the same mistake instead of letting it shape my identity.

Changing identities helped me understand Amanda Knox. Amanda Knox would never commit suicide. She would not die in a bunker, always running. What would she do? What would I do? I believed people were good, that men like Phil and Patrick were the norm, for better or worse. I dreamed the world was better than it seemed from my cell or my name's jail. I was extremely vulnerable while dreaming.

CHPATER 15
Ex-Conned

Media—traditional and social—taught me not to trust strangers with my private life. Foxy Knoxy was catnip to creeps who enjoyed debating whether it was worth risking being murdered to fuck me, creeps who propositioned me for murder-themed porn, and reporters who continued to comment on my sex appeal and asked their audiences, "Foxy Knoxy: Would Ya?" I wouldn't date or befriend somebody I didn't know before Italy. So when I joined social media, I avoided dating apps. No way, OkCupid! Tinder? The hell no. Facebook? The situation is difficult.

To my surprise, I was still in love. I didn't do it like other mid-20s folks in the mid-2010s. I didn't "go about" anything. I reunited with college boyfriend James. It happened fast. We'd been writing for years. Madison and I lived around the block from his place. For the first few months after moving in, I spent hours at his house listening to him play classical guitar. Now I was a loner like him. We lived together as hermits for two years. Till everything collapsed at once.

It was spring 2014. College graduation was near. I know most teens find this time bittersweet. You leave campus, friends, and teenage indiscretions. Start a career, build mature relationships, and be an adult. I had a special affinity with that university, making farewell difficult. It wasn't just that I graduated nearly twice as late as everyone else. University of Washington was my only familiar and safe environment after incarceration. I still got odd looks from classmates, but paparazzi couldn't follow me to university. That was also going gone.

No idea where to go or what to do. Madison moved cross-country. James and I split up. Re-convicted of murder, appealing a 28.5-year sentence, and facing extradition. Paparazzi were back, and tabloids were pleased to report that I was a "convicted killer" again. 2014 started poorly. It was now my worst year, rivaling 2009.

Madison wanted to drink with me before leaving. I didn't do it. I didn't want to be recognized, ogled like a freak show, or discreetly photographed. I also had strict orders from my lawyers: no pubs, karaoke, or parties. Until my troubles ended? Indefinitely? It was unclear. My second trial was character-based. The prosecution said I acted guilty, and a jury convicted me on empty allegations. I relied on appearances for my appeal and any extradition battle if it failed. A typical twenty-seven-year-old woman wasn't enough. I had to be invisible and perfect.

As lonely and anxious as I felt, I should have stayed home. I wanted to be normal. We visited a hip pub in town, which I had never been to. It was an underground dive beneath a burrito joint with sombreros, luchador masks, and tacky Jesus murals. It thrills. I kept my head down and avoided eye contact. Madison ordered for me. We drank whiskey sours and watched the crowd gesticulate in the red light over the loud music.

A younger man appeared unexpectedly. He sat at our table and inquired, "What are you two talking about so intently?"

Madison led. "None of your business."

He didn't recognize me and kept smiling. "No worries! Your conversation looked interesting. My friend recently got out of jail for something he didn't do, so I'm showing him a good time."

Our spirits rose. No way.

He phoned his Black friend, a lonely young man lying against the bar. Call him Mike. Mike walked over and sat across from me. A fit, beautiful man. He said hello distractedly.

"So what happened?" Madison inquired.

Mike's pal explained how he was released from jail after months of charges being dismissed. Mike rolled his eyes but smiled.

Are you okay? Asked him.

Looking away, he nodded. "Yeah, yeah," but I knew—or thought I knew—his look.

"I was in prison for something I didn't do, too," I said. Madison scowled at me.

Mike finally looked at me. "For what?"

I hesitated. "For murder."

"Holy shit!" exclaimed his pal. Mike just inspected me.

"I know what it's like when you first get out," I said. I informed him I still hand-washed underwear in the sink.

Madison and I spent the evening with Mike and his pal. After finishing our beers at the pub, we went to a café to hear amateur hip hop. We talked about Mike's "crazy" ex who accused him of various things as we went around the park. He served months in jail. He had to see a parole officer. His employment was gone. The man was broke. His relatives couldn't assist.

My gut wriggled. So many individuals helped me exit. Family welcomed me and housed me. Supporters raised $2,000 to help me recover. Mike had nobody to aid him, so I felt lucky.

Pay it forward was my goal. We met several times in the following weeks to walk and talk. Connected eventually. Was I his mentor or lover? He was my partner or project? It blurred. I believed I'd found someone who understood me. Beyond that, Mike allowed me to distract from my problems and make myself think I was better off. Caring for someone else with tangible hurdles like getting a phone or a job—problems I had addressed for myself and could immediately aid with—was a comfort. It made me joyful. I became blind.

Mike soon requested money. He said he couldn't afford his court-ordered psych evaluations. He received two grand from my legal fees savings.

A few weeks later, I introduced him to my family. My family held a cookout instead of a public college graduation ceremony to commemorate my graduation. I invited Mike. He immediately made my family feel awful. My friend drew me aside and warned, "Watch out. He's snakey." I was shocked that my friends and relatives wouldn't give another wrongfully accused individual the benefit of the doubt. Didn't he deserve? Did I?

I started arranging a cross-country move soon after the meeting. I followed Madison to New York, another impulsive decision. Our Harlem flats were close. It was my only plan. I asked my publisher for an internship one day at their building. I was offered freelance job reading slush pile novels. Like my past professions, money was low, but it started. I was in NYC and had a beginning in the arts. Despite being a convicted killer facing extradition, I had to stay cheerful and even enthusiastic. I hated being powerless. I feared relapsing into that dulled despair I knew so well. A odd, overwhelming mix of feelings.

Mike showed up on my doorway during all this. I invited him to start again in New York since he kept hitting hurdles in Seattle. I volunteered to house him until he found work and an apartment.

But Mike didn't look for work. He bought a Game Boy with the money I lent him for professional attire. He spent all day on my couch playing Pokémon. Madison, who was wary of Mike from the outset, urged me to fire him. She checked his arrest record and found domestic violence and burglary charges. She questioned: Was he wrongfully accused? Was that a lie?

I saw an old school acquaintance who relocated to New York years ago to pursue a music career a few days later. Mike heard us talking on the sidewalk from my apartment and walked up and hit my friend across the face. Like he slapped me. This is when I realized how severely I messed up.

I dragged Mike back to my flat and made him pack and go. He declined. I insisted. His friend, who introduced us, lived in D.C. "Go stay with him," I said. I gave him $200 for a train ticket and left.

Mike was on my bed when I got home from work two days later. He broke into my apartment from the fire escape.

Screamed.

He grabbed me.

I escaped his hands and ran.

His chase took me down four flights of stairs and into the street.

I jumped into a taxi, pleading, "Go!" Drive anywhere! Please!"

I couldn't visit Madison's flat. It was too close, and Mike knew her address. I panicked. My two cats might have escaped when I fled, leaving the door open. My darker imagination feared Mike might hurt them to get revenge at me. Madison advised me to call the police, but I was afraid of the consequences. Instead, I called my lawyers and described everything. They verified my suspicions. They said not to call the cops. If I did, the tabloids would report that I had dated a man who had been convicted of burglary and abusive against women. I only recognized Mike's true identity when they explained it. He was not a victim of an overzealous justice system like me. He was a liar, conman, burglar, and criminal like Rudy Guede.

Each hair on my body stood on end. If anyone found out, it would destroy my appeal and any chance of resisting extradition to serve my 28.5-year sentence in the U.S. I needed aid but didn't know how. I contacted my Seattle stepdad. He vowed to be on the following red-eye to New York City after I sobbed into the phone in shame.

The next morning, we returned to my apartment. Besides my pets, who thankfully hadn't fled, it was empty. When we entered the kitchen, we heard a creak. Mike was hiding behind the door as we turned around. The whole thing took seconds. Mike ran as my stepdad said, "Get the fuck out of here!" We immediately packed my stuff, and I flew back to Seattle, tail between my knees.

I felt terrible about my stupidity on the journey home. I missed the warnings. I ignored my relatives. They'd have to save me again. My new adult life in New York ended early. My publishing internship, which led to a writing career, ended. The instability of my existence extinguished my optimism. I tried so much to see the good in people and use my pain to help others, but it simply made me a target.

I tortured myself over this for years. My family graciously never irritated me. I did it for them. I should have known better after all my mistreatment. I hadn't realized that my naïve optimism, though vulnerable, was a strength, that we all make mistakes under pressure, and that feeling lost can obscure our vision. Never had I felt so lost.

With the world continuing saying my erroneous conviction was my fault, I wondered if it was real. I was stupid girl who made bad choices and wandered into risky situations, risking my life and those I loved. Maybe I deserved this mess of a life no one sensible would choose.

CHAPTER 16
We Know

Many forms of loneliness have crossed my path. Living in a book is calm and cozy. I used to climb my backyard tree, sit on a branch, and read Harry Potter for hours on summer afternoons. I was lonely in Perugia, walking great distances, discovering new stores and perspectives, pleased to be alone in an unfamiliar place yet longing for the familiar even though I knew I couldn't have both. A planetarium's unnerving surge when the lens zooms out and the Earth disappears into the Milky Way evokes the loneliness of feeling little and insignificant. Abandonment loneliness. I first witnessed it when I was fifteen, walked in on my oma crying hysterically into the phone, imploring her husband to return to his family after two years apart. Of all, loneliness was my constant companion in Capanne, where I was stripped of my life and surrounded by strangers from unimaginable backgrounds.

I wanted familiarity when I got home. I most wanted to return to my life before being wrongfully accused of murder. I did the only thing I could—return to school and join my friends.

The University of Washington wasn't what I remembered. All my pals graduated. While older than most of my classmates, I had more life experience but no wisdom from processing it. I felt weird and uneasy again, like the new kid on the cellblock.

Like in prison, I kept to myself. Enter, exit. As the teacher's pet, I raised my hand and engaged in class, but I ran when the bell rang. No lunch at the student hub, no evening campus hangouts, no extracurriculars, no buddies. Google Alerts alerted me when my classmates took secret photos of me in the lecture hall and shared them to social media with descriptions like "Foxy Knoxy" or "Look who's in my math class!" How should I proceed? I want to pee in her butt, but any other ideas?

In Capanne, I signed all my letters "Io lo so che non sono sola anche quando sono sola." Even alone, I know I'm not alone. Jovanotti's Italian rap song gave me the phrase. It became a mantra, connecting me to my family, friends, and the life I imagined outside.

The motto failed in freedom. Despite having family and friends, I felt more lonely than I thought. My lifelong home, my identity, was condemned. I became impatient and aggressive or terribly sad and withdrawn after 10 minutes of informal chat at family gatherings due to off-the-cuff remarks or celebrity gossip. Everything fell off my back before Capanne. My hypersensitivity and tendency to go off and shut off made me a land mine. My mom witnessed me alternate between fury, sadness, and apathy over seemingly minor things like being coaxed to drink a martini I didn't want or witnessing someone read People magazine. My mom wanted to help, but my family didn't understand. They couldn't. Trauma had shaped them differently than me. Different lessons were learned. Scuba diving through mankind seemed like being an alien living form unsuited to the environment. Who could comprehend my suffering?

Then I shared a poetry writing and Shakespeare literature class with the same girl. Even across the room, I felt connected to her. We gave comprehensive criticism in our writing session and fully experienced our characters while reading Shakespeare aloud.

She asked, "Want to meet this weekend to talk poetry?" I hesitated. She didn't seem to know who I was, but I was still told secrets in class and trailed by cameras outside my apartment. Yes, I risked suggesting an off-the-beaten-path café in my area.

Southern Seattle's Panama Hotel and Café is a historic landmark on the International District's fringe. Japanese Americans hid in the basement during WWII to avoid imprisonment. The hotel is still open, but I've never stayed there. I spent too much time in the ground-floor café. It had a broad range of tea and espresso, but most of all, it was peaceful and filled with odd tables, desks, seats, and couches, perfect for a laptop nook. I let my classmate inside my shelter.

We met every Saturday morning to discuss class, critique each other's poems, and socialize while writing for several weeks. Our poems were emotive and abstract. Despite not writing about prison or being wrongfully accused, my metaphors eventually evoked such topics. For whatever reason, her poems and mine resonated. In our writing, we tried to find meaning in feeling trapped and helpless. Even in my daydreams, I thought she was becoming my friend.

However, one Saturday morning, she sat next to me and said, "You're Amanda Knox."

My heart dropped. My throat dried. What did she Google? She thought she knew what? How would she treat me after I was so frank with her? Would she sell me newspapers like my neighbor? Would the Daily Mail publish my poor poems?

She touched my arm after seeing my distressed face. "Wait. Sorry. I meant I understand now. I know why we get along."

"You mean what?" I requested.

She leaned in and peered at me, gathering her words. Her voice lowered, she whispered, "I was raped when I was a teenager. Two I believed were buddies. I recognize the sensation of hopelessness that keeps appearing in your poetry."

When my heart started pounding again, I felt warm. She taught me a life-saving reality in an instant: you don't have to have lived the same experience to understand and connect with others. Part of me wondered if I wasn't doomed to loneliness.

Mom still believed in me. At my lowest, re-convicted and facing repatriation, she recognized my despair as a disease she couldn't fix. Someone else did. One day, Idaho Innocence Project director Dr. Greg Hampikian contacted her. Greg became involved in my case early on and issued an amicus brief—an expert DNA review—to help the American public believe in my innocence. Greg didn't ask about proof or law this time. The Innocence Network Conference, an annual gathering of all Innocence Projects nationwide, was in Portland later that month, he reminded my mom. Bring me there, he said. I was doubtful, but Mom was certain. I hated being in a room with hundreds of people who recognized me immediately. The idea horrified me. But Mom insisted. We drove three hours to Portland on a Friday afternoon in early April 2014.

A hotel conference center hosted the event in featureless rooms that likely housed real estate conventions and antique fairs on other weekends. We stopped at the double doors before the main ballroom after following signs. I looked at the tacky carpet. I had to clamp my teeth from sweating through my shirt and shivering. I was about to turn around and drive three hours back to Seattle when Mom unlocked those doors and nudged me inside.

A large area with banquet tables and largely guys was packed. They laughed and smiled. I felt like I'd come to someone else's family reunion. A lanky black man with short dreadlocks and a big white man with a military hairstyle saw me. They walked up to me. Fear was evident on my face. I was a convicted murderer. They needed to know. They had to know I didn't belong in this gathering of lawyers, scientists, and exonerees. I almost left despite their smiles. Would they like something from me? They hugged me one by one. When they saw my confusion, one said, "You don't have to explain a thing, little sister. We know."

Suddenly, tears fell. Sitting at an adjacent table, Antione Day and Josh Kezer told me their story. Each served nearly a decade for false crimes. Like many of the dozens of exonerees I would encounter in the coming days, they had followed my case religiously—just not in the way I expected. Many of them rejoiced when I was liberated, rooting for me from their prisons. One exoneree told me that if a calm suburban white girl could survive prison, so could they. Now, maybe people will pay attention when cops push innocents into accusing themselves and others behind closed doors, when they lie on the witness stand, and when prosecutors use junk science and character assassination.

Another life-saving revelation reached me instantly: my trauma was not unusual. People didn't have to explain themselves to me or vice versa. I mattered despite being a drop in the bucket.

This community loved me, but especially my mom. On the second day of the meeting, she was talking to Johnnie Savory, a thirty-year prisoner, who said he had never seen the ocean. She remarked, "Well then, let's go!" Right now! Why not? She pulled him by the arm, drove him to Oregon, and ran barefoot into the Pacific.

Weekends brought me a new family. A family of mostly guys, mostly men of color, who had rough life before their erroneous convictions. Not all exonerees I met were on death row. Most had served more prison time than I did. In prison, they lost loved ones. They were released into the world with little time to find love or start a family. I instantly felt lucky. At least I was free. Only four years, I could appeal.

After that weekend, I felt alive, eager to fight for my innocence, and most importantly, like I belonged. I had a new mission. I look different from most exonerees. In many ways, I'm unusual. Young, female, college-educated. My class didn't have to worry about the criminal justice system, so I never did before I was falsely accused. Translation was my goal when I studied a foreign language. I eventually became one, but not like I expected. Here, I convey this sensation, felt by many in our society, across cultural and economic lines.

Since that first Innocence Network Conference, I've spoken at dozens of local innocence projects from Alaska to Florida to promote awareness and funds. I tell them I'm not special. You can be wrongfully convicted without being strange or unlucky. You can withstand it and believe in the world's goodness without being brilliant or strong. Same for disease, violence, bankruptcy, etc. Face and overcome misfortune as part of being human. In the thick of it, it's easy to feel alone. Feeling cursed or blessed (fame and money may be lonely!) separates you from everyone else, causing loneliness. Lonely people say, You don't know what it's like. I told myself that many times. Each repetition expands the gap between you and the world. In that division, loneliness grows like a vine that returns no matter how hard you pull it. But the plant dies when you realize that others understand and that you're not alone in life. Though it may seem like it, you are not alone.

When well-meaning individuals remark, "I can't imagine what you've been through," I answer, "Try." Empathy may bridge the gap between us because we're all going through something and carrying something. Empathy is imagination-based. While you may not have experienced someone else's worst moment, you have. Being seen for who I am, my problems, and my goals is one of my greatest gifts. My exoneree family and the poetry class girl, who became my first true friend in freedom and remains close, gave me that gift.

However, I know that to accept this gift, you must be open to others and share your private life. I was reluctant to take that risk for a long time. No wonder I felt lonely. How many offerings and true connections had I missed? Strangely, my mantra came back when I took risks, were vulnerable, and admitted my loneliness.

Even when alone, I'm not alone.

CHAPTER 17
Sisterhood of Ill Repute

I was somewhat aware of the ancient notion that all women secretly detest each other and cannot be friends before Italy. Some call it "venimism" or "mean girls." The Italian criminologist Cesare Lombroso said in 1893 that, "Due to women's latent antipathy for one another, trivial events give rise to fierce hatreds; and due to women's irascibility, these occasions lead quickly to insolence and assaults Latent antipathy's cause? Sexual jealousy, yes. We detest each other because we compete for male attention.

I always believed this misogynistic notion was incorrect. My sisters, mom, and most girls I knew had girlfriends, including school and soccer girls. I thought my innocence was evident too. I was accused of murder and called a disgusting, drug-addled, woman-hating slut in my courtroom, where a cross hung on the wall and my Catholic prosecutor accused me.

Dr. Giuliano Mignini said Meredith was surprised Amanda started a relationship with a boy after arriving in Perugia and that she owned condoms and a vibrator. Meredith may have argued with Amanda because she brought strange males into the house. Amanda, perhaps intoxicated, wanted to include Meredith in a violent sex game. It was her chance to avenge that British girl who was too serious and 'moderate' for her liking, whose network of English friends consistently rejected her, and who publicly accused Amanda of being dirty and too friendly with men. Amanda must have believed it was time to avenge that "simpering goody two-shoes."

Dr. Giuliano Mignini admitted me into a not-so-secret society of women with these comments, which had global media coverage. You know who I mean. The women included in TMZ, SNL, and David Letterman's Top Ten Lists. Women dressed in Halloween costumes and referenced in rap lyrics. We treat women like punching bags and lines. Women whose shattered bodies, relationships, most vulnerable times, and worst experiences we devour like candy. This is the Sisterhood of Ill Repute. Before meeting Monica Lewinsky, I didn't realize I was in this club.

Just before my first speaking event at a private conference in Seattle in January 2017. Monica also spoke. I had an hour to kill and was afraid. I rehearsed six times before the event after perfecting my talk.

I went to the areas that hurt because I knew I had to break my heart in front of the public to convey my narrative. Standing in front of hundreds who might believe all kinds of lies about me was different from saying those remarks in my living room.

Monica invited me to her hotel room before the event to discuss.

She suffered the biggest public shame when I was a child. I remember hearing my family debate the news during dinner. It was my first time hearing the term "oral sex," and when I said I didn't understand why everyone was so concerned over people speaking romantic things over the phone, my family laughed. In the years that followed, I lazily assimilated the tabloid Monica image. If you had asked me about the tale in high school, I would have answered, "Oh, yeah, Monica." I didn't research it. The blowjob lady." I have yet to understand going from anonymous to "public figure."

After suffering tabloid treatment personally, I respectfully doubted I could trust the media's portrayal of anyone. When Monica gave her TED Talk, "The Price of Shame," she showed me and millions of others who Monica was and always was. I had followed her closely since then, reading all her Vanity Fair writing and feeling vindicated when she reported being relentlessly embarrassed in the press, humiliated, and demonized for others' enjoyment and political advantage.

I anticipated to be star-struck in that hotel room. A large sister appeared very immediately.

She was friendly and warm from the start. I had tea from her. Sitting by the windows overlooking downtown Seattle, we discussed my speech. She provided me great advice on mental preparation and self-care, but we really talked about trauma processing. How you're never done with it and how talking about it publicly triggers and heals. She described her successful and unsuccessful therapies and why. I've never met a more dedicated therapist. I think what wasn't expressed struck me most. You're that Italian gal! How was prison? What's fame like? All those cringey to insulting conversational notes that popped up when I met a stranger who thought they knew me from a decade of media coverage were gone. Not because Monica was unaware of everything. She asked Amanda for tea after reading about Foxy Knoxy like millions of others.

I left that meeting feeling seen. I had similar experiences with my poetry pal and at the Innocence Network Conference. I didn't have to explain the anguish of widespread public shame to this person. Since coming home, I had struggled with my place as a public figure—the invasion of my privacy, my inability to resist journalistic slander—but seeing her survive and thrive gave me faith that I could too. Empathy may unite people with drastically diverse life experiences, but it's easier when the other person has been in your shoes. Support groups exist, and I left that gathering encouraged to connect with other publicly shamed women.

My podcast, The Truth about True Crime, included a live episode with Lorena Bobbitt (now Gallo) at a true crime convention in Washington, D.C. Lorena, like Monica, had fled irreparable reputational damage for twenty years. But she consented to meet me on stage and chat to a live audience about our lives in public shame. Most people remember John Wayne Bobbitt's castration, but they forget that Lorena was a victim of domestic violence and marital rape and committed her own violent deed while mentally unstable. This doesn't excuse her conduct, but it's important context typically left out.

Lorena and I promoted that event at a local TV news station the morning of. A New Jersey comedian entered while I was waiting for Lorena in the green room. We briefly chatted after his on-air part. I told him I was interviewing Lorena, and he said, "What about?" Which knife slice sausage best?

"No," I answered. "Actually, we'll be talking about how people still reduce her to a penis-chopping joke when she is a complex human being who advocates for domestic violence victims."

Thankfully, the comedian said, "Oh, I get it. She's not evil. I am!"

As accountable as we are for the media we consume, I don't want to vilify the audience, the millions of us who carelessly accepted twisted and incomplete stories about Lorena, Monica, and me. Such stories exploit our worst inclinations. We will always find judgment easier than kindness, understanding, forgiveness, and a sophisticated grasp of the intricacy behind most significant damages. It feels nice to detest "bad" people, especially "bad women." The "mean girl," "homewrecker," and "girl-on-girl" crime stories are thrilling because they support the assumption that women are each other's worst adversaries. Amanda vs. Meredith. It distracts from men's crimes against women and validates them, allowing males to despise women.

Modern times have far surpassed Salem, 1692. We've all mastered witch-burning. We can dox, shame, and deplatform targets instantly on social media without due process or proportionality. We all, including me, are at risk by posting about our dinners, treks, and marriage proposals. We choose that daily without thinking. Never wanted to be a public figure, but I made a Myspace page in high school and a Facebook page in college. When I was on trial, my social media sites were mined for vilification material. The tabloids found my soccer nickname, "Foxy Knoxy," and a photo of me pretending to fire a Gatling gun at a war museum. As Monica was patient zero of the 24-hour news cycle and internet shame, I was patient zero of social media cancellation.

The social media algorithms that amplify indignation are a large part of the problem, but we also need to expect greater standards from traditional media, which often fails to contextualize a story, even if it is correct in detail. I realized this when I compared my tale to Monica's. What you call matters. The "Lewinsky scandal" that led to President Bill Clinton's impeachment was called so for years. Who committed adultery and lied? Who exploited whom and why? What about Ken Starr? Calling it the "Lewinsky scandal" instead of the "Clinton affair" or "Starr investigation" absolves these individuals. People call the events in Perugia that ruined my life the "sordid Amanda Knox saga" instead of "the murder of Meredith Kercher by Rudy Guede." This framing cements my guilt, exonerates Rudy Guede, and erases Meredith as a victim.

I can only do so much to correct these erroneous frames, but my impotence to do so and stop traditional media and online talk has been a blessing. I understood my reputation and public self aren't mine. Socially and legally, that has always been true. My fame is public property. As is yours. It still hurts when someone publicly shames or disparages you. We value our reputations because losing your tribe's trust is death. Honesty, reliability, safety, and friendliness matter most. How your bank balance matters matters. It shapes life prospects. But it doesn't reveal your true self. Your reputation isn't yours forever. Others can shape, alter, or destroy it without consequence.

I learned to ignore others' opinions because they made me miserable. This was brought home to me when Netflix published the documentary about my case and advertised it with two photographs of me with the words "monster" and "victim" on them. These commercials were everywhere online and on huge L.A. and New York billboards. In Times Square, pedestrians passed past me under those huge photos of my face, unaware.

I realized that my public persona was like a piñata, and I watched as people joyfully swung at it from the rear of the throng. My genuine self wasn't in the spotlight. The real me was a sister, daughter, foreign language and dance enthusiast, Renaissance nerd, and theater geek, eating an heirloom tomato and kissing the dish. My true self was impenetrable.

Monica saw my true self when we met. People ask me about being acquainted with Monica Lewinsky. It's like actual friendship. Like having a huge sister. Our past traumas and present challenges—a harsh news report, my legal saga—are public. Beyond that, you know better. Monica has texted me on more than one bad day to check in on my mental health when I was too busy to breathe.

I'm not the first woman to receive a scarlet letter, and I won't be the last. The scene within my Sisterhood of Ill Repute comforts me. From this perspective, crucifying others for their sins, real or imagined, reveals more about the shamer than the shamed. I am hopeful that we may all become less likely to piñata our fellow people. It seemed unimaginable that smoking would be virtually unanimously condemned as poisonous and ugly. Doctors once smoked while evaluating kids. Gen Z is changing sugary sodas and alcohol. Our culture can recognize harmful behaviors and push them to the margins and replace them with healthier ones, albeit we may never eliminate them. Shame-fueled media follows suit. Changes are already evident.

Kentucky lawyers attended my seminar years ago. Later, a woman my age approached me. She was crying and had trouble speaking.

"I'm sorry," she said. "I regret entertaining you."

I hugged her deeply. No more women-hating.

CHAPTER 18
Just Amanda

While my peers were dating at their peak, I was isolated from flirtation, romance, and sex. I was rusty at all social interactions when I went home, but I was a romance rookie when they locked me up. Finding a healthy romantic life in freedom was difficult after being imprisoned for a sex crime known worldwide as rapist and killer. I didn't know who I could trust to tell TMZ my personal life. Raffaele went on a date with a female who turned out to be an Italian tabloid journalist the next day.

I was greatly disturbed by Mike in 2014. I let someone I didn't know into my intimate life because I thought he was like me, had the same problems, and could solve the world together. My need to be understood made me a great con victim. I felt ashamed and scared. I stopped trusting my instincts. I thought romance was not for me. I had nearly forgotten what it was like to feel gorgeous in a cute sundress, make eyes with a guy across the room at a party, and navigate the awkward, exciting, and sometimes upsetting dance of sex. Most of all, I missed company.

Enter Colin. Colin and I were middle school classmates but lost touch in college. From New York, he sought to become David Bowie. Seattle was my home before I went to Italy. Although we didn't know each other as adults, I recognized the nice, smart, safe person from years ago when we reconnected.

Colin the adult was gorgeous, thoughtful, and fun. I liked him most because he was safe. I saw in him a guy who would never exploit, deceive, or mistreat me, and though I didn't realize it, I thought that was the most I could expect for as "the girl accused of murder."

Our bond grew throughout my late 2014 dilemma, when I was talking to my counsel about turning myself in and resisting extradition. Colin rode with us. After watching the case from afar, he defended me as a martyr for injustice as the newspapers painted me as a killer.

I accepted his proposal after months of dating. As I faced extradition, holding onto this symbolic link to my home life seemed like magic, as if it would protect me from Italian prison. I said sure, but I was hesitant. Colin said I was Joan of Arc reincarnated, and I wondered if he knew me well. Not a femme fatale, but no saint. I was a normal girl who made mistakes. I didn't want quasi-religious iconography or my worst experience to define me.

I was confronting an extreme form of a common love dilemma. It begins when you swipe right or see someone across the room. You imagine all the ways they could meet your needs. In the fluttery early days of a relationship, confirmation bias makes you magnify that shoulder rub in the park and ignore his rudeness to the waiter at dinner. Imagine a person and fall in love with them. You're dissatisfied when the person's stubbornness shatters that idea. You changed. My lover—where is she? you think, unaware that individual never lived. You split, meet someone new, and repeat.

Colin and I both fell for this. He was in love with a fictional martyr. I fell in love with a man who I believed knew me from childhood but hardly did.

Every time these misgivings surfaced, I pushed them back down. I thought I was lucky to have anyone because I could be imprisoned next week. Colin waited with me on March 27, 2015, for my second appeal verdict. I still expected them to maintain my conviction and force me to leave my family the next morning. I couldn't picture the court acquitting Raffaele and myself, ending our legal nightmare.

My legal emancipation took months. As my life possibilities grew, so did my incompatibility with Colin. Instead of calling off the engagement and breaking up, which would have been healthier for both of us, I clutched on because I loved Colin and convinced myself I couldn't anticipate a deeper relationship. Colin wasn't to blame. My fault for falling for the Hallmark love myth.

A bizarre twist of fate: I had been writing for the local newspaper for over a year and was finally using my byline post-exoneration when I was requested to review War of the Encyclopaedists, a novel by two local writers. It was touching, funny, smart, and dumb in the appropriate ways. I wrote a great review and sent it to my editor, and that was it. But then I left my apartment and saw a banner in a café window promoting a book launch party for that novel at my neighborhood bookstore that evening! After being hunted, I avoided public gatherings, but it was so coincidental that I felt like taking a chance.

A few minutes before the event, I entered Elliott Bay Book Company's basement reading room, thinking I could watch quietly and secretly from the back. Instead of a solemn literary reading, I found a lively gathering of over 100 people drinking wine and beer in that room. It was celebratory and exciting, with just front-row seats available.

Right away, murmurs began. I felt confined when I saw others pointing and watching, but the reading took away that feeling. The authors were an unusual couple on stage. One was a stocky, bald army veteran and the other a hipster Elton John. They were best friends with obvious chemistry.

I was too shy to ask questions during the Q&A or wait in line to get my book signed, so I asked for an interview afterward.

The following week, I met Chris Robinson and Gavin Kovite at Chris's apartment for a professional interview about co-authoring a novel and navigating the fuzzy boundary between memoir and fiction, which turned into a scotch tasting. After talking about space travel, we started watching Star Trek: The Next Generation. I soon realized we were just hanging out. Strangely, it felt natural and comfortable because I didn't know these two guys.

I had many chances to leave in the evening, but I stayed. Chris, who had a serious relationship, was going with Gavin to see a woman he found on OkCupid to keep it casual. Tagged along too. The woman house-sat a Capitol Hill mansion where the four of us hung together. That evening felt like a dream: being in someone else's house, examining their things, spending time with old friends who had earned my trust, talking about art, literature, and philosophy, being Amanda, not "the girl accused of murder."

That evening, I photographed Chris and Gavin in goofy poses. Wine was consumed while we made up stories about the mansion residents. Chris and I had a serious talk as Gavin flirted with the other female. Chris was funny, quick to laugh, contemplative, erudite, vulnerable, and uninterested in small talk. He asked me about my engagement to Colin. Was I ready? Was I anxious? Though I should have asked myself these questions, I realized I didn't have the answers. I realized I wasn't ready and wasn't convinced I was on the proper road. I told Chris about my doubts, and he told me about his despair from years before, his obsession with suicide, and how he was still a Romantic nihilist. He said, "Life has no inherent meaning, but there's still beauty, and that's enough." He read Wallace Stevens poems. Quoted Wu-Tang Clan lyrics. He asked about my life, family, hopes, and goals, but never Italy or prison. We parted ways on the street at midnight. Chris clasped my hand and Gavin hugged me like a bear. "This was so much fun," he said. "We should friends." I had a premonition when he let go of my hand. As I walked back to my apartment through the warm summer night, I felt the same assurance as when the sun rose: I could love that man.

Chris didn't win my heart that night. I scarcely know him. Still engaged. I met his lovely serious girlfriend at the reading. I expected our lives to diverge. I knew deep down that Chris and I might be madly in love in another universe.

My night ended with a sense of blessed and unexpected normalcy. The first time since escaping from my mental condition as a prey animal hunted by forces much greater and stronger than myself, I thought, Wow. Can I just make friends now? Like a normal person? Not just uncommon trauma bonds like my poetry classmate, but anyplace, with anyone?

Over the next six months, Chris and I maintained in touch but rarely saw each other. He and Gavin spent a month in Detroit researching Deliver Us, their next work. Colin and I grew apart. Chris returned to Seattle devastated after his girlfriend broke up with him in Detroit. My shoulder was available for crying. Chris and Gavin spent two months at Yaddo, a Saratoga Springs writer's retreat, that fall. Colin and I separated then. Not because of Chris. Instead of safe and reactive, Chris showed me the possibilities of an exciting, forward-looking connection. That potential was the final straw that ended my relationship with Colin. Chris outgrew his post-breakup malaise after returning from Yaddo with a fresh novel draft. He invited me to cook dinner and watch a movie I suggested. He made artichoke risotto—I had no idea he could cook—and we watched the movie. Chris wrapped his arm around me halfway, which was nice. He slowly stroked the inside of my palm with his finger as I bent my arm to grab his hand, the most constrained yet erotic moment of my life. Six months after we started dating, Chris and I moved in. Already I knew he would be my husband and father. From our first meeting, Chris gave me a gift I thought I'd never receive. Tabloid stories didn't interest him. He wanted to know me uniquely. Once they discovered he knew me, everyone asked him, "Do you think she did it?" Is she weird? He rejected that degrading mentality and made a dramatic decision: he refused to Google me or read any media coverage of me. Despite not following the case, he understood there was a lot of misinformation regarding the evidence and debate. He didn't want that lens to alter his vision of me. He calmly discussed the case and incarceration when I asked, but never forced me to. He offered me the gift of allowing me be myself after years of feeling trapped in my life and the public image of me. Not a symbol, target, celebrity, or villain—just Amanda.

CHAPTER 19
Punching Down

Not often do I meet someone harsh in person. I'm proud that when people meet me in person, they see me for who I am. I normally face negativity from afar. I get tabloid criticism for clicks. Never-met haters vent in the comments. I delete and block like Whac-A-Mole.

Good days, though. I'm not always perfect. When the Daily Mail called my talk to law students crude, it hit me. They had the Kerchers' lawyer call to say my speaking was inappropriate. Although I promoted criminal justice reform, I was the villain.

I thought about this at my sister's birthday comedy club against my better judgment. We crowded into a booth at the back to watch her favorite comedian. The first comic got the crowd going by saying he couldn't be happier now that white and black girls have huge bottoms. Despite my terrible mood and the vulgar joke, I laughed. As I sipped my chardonnay, I relaxed. I said this would be fun. Who knew I needed a comedy club night? Another local opening preceded the headliner, and I recognized him when he took the stage. From where did I know him? After a few jokes, he asked, "Have you ever been in a room with a famous person and you didn't realize it?" I came out in a cold sweat when my neck tingled.

People recognize me. People approach me in airports, grocery stores, and restaurants. Lacking context, folks struggle to locate me. "Were we high school classmates? You look familiar." I tell them who I am sometimes and don't always. "Just one of those faces," I remark. I take use of anonymity opportunities.

I appreciate when the spotlight isn't on me, so I was happy when two local comedians requested Chris to be interviewed for a podcast about his novel a few months before this night at the comedy club. I sat silently in the corner recording. My cross-stitch creation for Chris's birthday was a Super Mario Bros. scenario.

One comic brought Chris down the hall to show him the lavatory after the interview, and I showed the other comic my gift. He apparently didn't recognize me. He saw me as his girlfriend. He liked my cross-stitch project and we chatted about video games for a while.

We packed things and departed after Chris returned. Talking to the comic wasn't memorable, but it was fun. Friendly small talk, which I don't like when it turns into, "Holy hell, you were convicted of what?" The stage comic didn't forget it, but I would have.

"Have you ever been in a room with a celebrity and discovered it later? His girlfriend joined me for my podcast interview. She's knitting in the corner all the time."

I felt a panic attack as my breath quickened. Still, I hoped his joke wouldn't be about me. Some part of me liked that he unwittingly repeated this joke's premise. He was again in my room without recognizing it.

After, my friend asks, 'What did you think of Amanda?' 'She's hot, sure.' He then asks, "Dude, you didn't recognize her?" It was Amanda Knox.

My three sisters then looked at my ghost-white face. The only silent table was ours.

"I said, 'You left me in a room with Amanda Knox?! There were knitting needles! She could have killed me! That's like locking me up with O. J.

All the tables laughed. I remained paralyzed until his set ended, trying to control my breathing and not cry. Both sisters tried to calm me calmly. My birthday girl sister was furious. She left the table and called me to the hallway five minutes later. She shit-talked her way back to the green room to demand the comic apologize. It was my worst wish, but she was upset, it was her birthday, and she wouldn't accept no.

He looked sad approaching the club entrance. My sister gave it to him. He apologized weakly and said comics seek everywhere for material. It was a joke. I laugh about my autistic cousins." I felt trapped, unsure what to say.

My sister requested he remove that joke from his set—he had another show a few hours later. I started crying when we returned to our seats. Staying for the headliner was impossible.

My sister's friend told us that the comic repeated his joke in the second set and made fun of her that night. How many times had he repeated that joke? How many open mics in my hometown had he perfected his wording? After calming down, I spent hours trying to find out why his joke hurt me. Many comedians had made fun of me. Even Bill Hader impersonated me on SNL. Not one joke was kind. This seemed like water off my back.

Sadness dominated my mood. This event proved that a pleasant face-to-face conversation would not silence the Hitchcock soundtrack playing in people's thoughts when they heard my name. I knew this wasn't the last time my worst experience was someone else's joke. Casey Anthony, Jodi Arias, or Amanda Knox?

I've always enjoyed comedy. I know comedians must challenge boundaries, always walking up to the line and sometimes crossing it. As bizarre as it is to have my worst experience made into a comedy, I understand why comedians do it. Their ailment is so common it has no name. I call it 2D-osis—seeing people as cardboard cutouts. Our predecessors never had to deal with more than a few hundred people in their small communities, so it's hard to imagine anyone beyond our immediate families, friends, and colleagues as genuine. It's why meeting your elementary school teacher at the grocery store is so shocking. She shops? And eats? How could she exist outside the classroom? Thanks to social media, most people we see daily are in 2D. Photos and concepts of people we connect with superficially, parasocially, and quasi-anonymously.

I know many people only know me from a tabloid murder scandal. That context persists because 2D-osis is easier than envisioning the guy who cuts you off in traffic—his extended family, hopes and worries, and nice things he says to his daughter when he tucks her in at night. I struggle too. Remembering that helps me forgive those who hurl darts at Amanda Knox cardboard cutouts.

It also helps me laugh at myself. In the last hours of the 2020 Biden-Trump election, I tweeted, "Whatever happens, the next four years can't be as bad as that four-year study abroad I did in Italy, right?" Tens of thousands praised it, but some labeled me crass and insensitive. "Delete this for your dignity." "This stinks." "You absolute ghoul."

I get this when I laugh about my erroneous conviction. I understand their anger. For some of them, I'm guilty, and any statement about my experience is like O. J. Simpson joking about getting away with murder. Some think I'm joking about Meredith's murder since they know my name. I laugh about my own experiences, but they don't understand. I joke about bogus accusations and jail time. After losing everything, my sense of humor helps me cope.

Comedy has immense power, therefore it's no surprise that comedians are often people who've suffered serious loss. Comedy lets us own what's been taken from us and give it a significance beyond sadness.

Prodding your wounds and expecting a jolt but getting a tickling is cathartic.

The best jokes highlight real truths and offer a unique viewpoint. Dimensionalize rather than flatten their subjects. This is especially true for self-deprecating comedians. Unpacking their flaws, shortcomings, and scars makes them more human, and we feel more seen in their paintings. It's a service. The self-deprecating comedian becomes a martyr, reassuring viewers. Together, we face life's challenges.

So I lean in. If people keep comparing me to O. J. Simpson, I should joke about it.

What unites Foxy Knoxy with O. J.?

They share the same birthday as Tom Hanks.

I don't believe in astrology because of it!

CHAPTER 20
Joy

While I was in prison and on trial, Chris was in PhD school and touring the country as a bohemian writer, living in artist colonies. His life seemed so different from mine at first. His twenties were spent in a lifestyle different from his friends. His job was unstable. He spent months with strangers or no one, hundreds of miles from his friends and family. He read as many books as I did in prison over four years, and while I sent innumerable letters to friends and family, he published several poetry collections, two novels, and dozens of short stories and articles. Writing helped him digest his life, like me. He also contemplated suicide in his loneliest moments on his aimless, self-created lyrical odyssey.

Chris was perfectly positioned to appreciate my baggage into our partnership.

Remember the fish who said, "What the hell's water?" That was my fear. I stopped noticing it after swimming and breathing it for so long. What would I have responded if you had asked me if I was terrified post-exoneration? No one pursues me anymore." I was still cautious, watchful, and ready to be scrutinized after years of living under a harsh spotlight where my every eccentricity was magnified and cast in a frightening light. Was that sensible, as I told myself, or my prison?

In the summer of 2017, Chris and I started packing for Burning Man, which raised this concern.

Chris and I played together from the start. I organized a cyberpunk LARP scavenger hunt for his birthday. Chris built an American Gladiator-style obstacle course in our park for my birthday. We anticipated every costume party. We dressed as Star Trek characters for Chris's brother's Seattle Knights sword-fighting theater company's Viking-themed party. While everyone was dressed in leather and fur and drinking mead from elk-horn mugs, Chris and I scanned them with our tricorders.

Chris indulged my playful side, letting me rediscover joy, something I was told was banned. He then decided to create a novel set at Burning Man and invited us for "research." Don't tell me Amanda Knox "found herself" at Burning Man. I didn't. Strangely, it arrived at the correct time on my journey. They say the playa provides.

After packing tons of water, food, sunscreen, sun hat, goggles, and dust mask, Chris and I went to Goodwill to locate our Burning Man clothes. He found XL sequined clothes on the women's aisle. I paused when I saw a semi-transparent leotard. If a "All You Need Is Love" tee made the news media clutch their pearls, what would happen if someone recognized me? After nearly returning it to the rack, I realized I was surrendering to my fear again and put it in my basket.

I was immediately transported by Black Rock City. Simpler terms: 80,000 people in tents and RVs in the desert. However, that description hardly grasped Burning Man's allure, which was an ethereal, almost mythic city that arose for 10 days and then vanished like one of Italo Calvino's Invisible Cities. No money, trade, or barter existed. A gift economy only. Strangers offered me a water bottle spritz, shoulder rub, handmade pickles, and pho soup. Chris and I had picked a few baskets of plums from our backyard, and that gift—fresh fruit in the desert when most people were eating dehydrated meals—brought pure joy to people.

Everyone was welcome at Burning Man. Loud techno dance parties didn't suit me, and I've never been a night owl. Instead, I rode my bike through the peaceful streets in the scorching sun while millions slept after their nightlife revelry and encountered several delights.

I saw a bunny parade fight a carrot march. I watched cat videos on repeat in a large pillow-filled tent. In a two-hour Ask Me Anything with a physicist and mathematician, I asked, "What the heck is time, anyway?" I left the heat for a camp with chardonnay and painting tools. I reflected on my fear and let it inspire watercolor works. Chris and I Lindy We rode bikes across the flat playa like tiny neon fish in an unfathomable abyss after hopping into the twilight at one camp.

After three days at Burning Man, I was dirty, fatigued, energized, and confused. No one recognized me. I wore a dust mask and goggles most of the time, and our friends started calling me Domu, like a Miyazaki guide. While my buddies changed their minds, I stayed sober, advising us to stay hydrated and guiding us back to camp through dust storms.

People around me had far lower inhibitions. I passed the Human Carcass Wash, Burning Man's only place to get clean. After rotating through the carwash-like stations as a human soaper, scrubber, rinser, and dryer, you were allowed to strip naked and walk through the cleansing gauntlet. On day four, I braved the see-through leotard. It was little compared to what others wore, but it was rebellion for me. As a child, I didn't feel shame about my physique, but the media made me afraid to wear a bikini at the beach. A part of me always thought,

Don't give them any reason to think you're a slut! I was sick of hearing my fearful inner voice.

That day, I found a geodesic dome hosting Slutty Storytelling, an open mic where individuals told their most embarrassing, wicked, and titillating sex stories. My terrified inspiration led me to jump in front of the throng and tell them how I learnt to masturbate in prison. A pleasant light slowed my rushing heart.

Judgement, like advertising and transactional relationships, is a major component of our daily air. (These three aspects are prevalent at grocery store checkout tabloids). I knew that Burning Man was a bubble in the capitalist world I lived in every other day and could only be sustained by a massive influx of time, energy, and money (tickets cost nearly six hundred dollars), and that it lasted only ten days, a shimmering ephemeral city that could never sustain itself. I realized that Burning Man's worth was in experiencing a world without transactions, shame, or judgment for a few days.

The shard of anguish in my chest, mirroring my anxiety, sadness, and rage, kept nibbling at me. I was free now, right? No one was trying to put me back in a cell. Why was I scared? I knew what hurt me in Italy. At Burning Man, structures like the stories-tall Man sculpture are not the only ones to catch fire. Thousand of burners visit the Temple throughout week, leaving keepsakes and tokens. There were many images of deceased loved ones, messages, flowers, and little souvenirs like earrings and baseball mitts with unique meaning solely to the deceased. A man wrote a hand-scrawled confession saying he raped someone and wanted to kill himself. A bride fastened her garment to a beam. A photo of a tiny child made me wonder if he had died or gone from a playground.

My small watercolor postcard from the Art and Chardonnay camp went in the Temple. It said, "Pain was simpler in prison." On Sunday night, it burned alongside all the other sacred artifacts while the throng sat silently and cried for themselves, everyone, and the possibility of finally letting go.

Play is poisoned by anxiety, especially judgment. Play is a wiggle hands, not a fist. It involves looseness and risk-taking. Over the year, Chris and I played more as I let go of my trepidation after Burning Man. Our clothes became increasingly wacky, spectacular, and color-coordinated as we danced on subway stations and sang in the grocery store.

In late fall 2018, a meteorite hit our property on a Sunday night. It appeared that way. Chris couldn't keep a straight expression; he was planning. Hidden speakers in the yard played E.T. music as I warily approached the smoldering, shimmering crater. The meteorite included a shining slab of iridescent stone with an Encyclopedia Galactica entry about us, our love, and our future.

"It appears to be some kind of data crystal," Chris advised.

I laughed. It's data crystal. Okay, what?"

"Oh my god." Chris stated. I was thinking about this, but it happened already. In the future? It's occurring now?"

Chris kneeled. "Will you stay with me until the last star in the last galaxy burns out, and beyond? Will Amanda Marie Knox marry me?

It takes time to register. I was stunned. With its sci-fi special effects and exquisite execution, this moment was my person. I wanted this life.

Finally, I muttered, "Uh... yeah."

Chris and I wrote our wedding story based on his preparations, as usual. We envisioned a performance-escape chamber. At our wedding, 200 individuals would participate in a romantic live-action Doctor Who episode.

Our time travel–themed wedding was on February 29, 2020, after a year of crafting props, sets, and puzzles. The elderly venue manager called me into the office the day before as we quickly assembled the scenery and tested the AV. "I think I made a mistake," he murmured. "Some journalists called to ask if we were having a wedding tomorrow. Yes, I said. My mind was blank. I didn't say your name, but I probably gave it away.

I froze inside. "Okay. I stuttered, "Please don't say anything else." Returning to the wedding hall dazed, I approached Chris. We have a problem."

I wept. I knew what would happen. Paparazzi would photograph us. They may annoy visitors or enter the wedding location. Everyone came in period and futuristic costumes. A stranger may sneak in easily. Their latest scoop would be framed like this: "Narcissistic Knox Holds Bizarre Celebration While Kerchers Grieve." My every success was interpreted as an awful insult to Meredith. It was clear: How dare I exist without her?

I clutched my heart again. It wasn't simply that they labeled me a tragic figure and expected me to mourn forever. It was also that I secretly agreed with them. Part of me felt guilty that I survived my study abroad but she didn't. I blended my identity and tragedy with Meredith's. I was still angry, wounded, and sad because I and she could never be that courageous, stupid, dreamy-eyed kid who boarded that airplane to Italy.

I hyperventilated. Chris embraced me. "We'll get wristbands and security guards, check phones at the door, and solve this problem," he said. Even if we don't, look at this! We looked around the ballroom we'd transformed over the last week—the glowing time tunnel guests would enter through, the smoking regeneration canisters onstage we would emerge from instead of walking down the aisle, and the dozens of funny clocks we'd built on the walls, their hands spinning erratically. "You deserve to enjoy this," he continued. "You deserve joy. Do not let them steal that."

Weddings really do fly by. Our friends and family dressed as ancient Rome, sixteenth-century France, Hollywood, the distant future, and even a dinosaur. A lightsaber duel, hectic escape room puzzle hour, wild dancing, Prohibition Era cocktails, and Viking mead. Our wedding was shortly before the pandemic shutdown, so everyone called it "the last fun thing."

As Chris and I collapsed in bed that night, weary from excitement, I felt like I did in that safe home the night I was freed from prison—fearful of falling asleep and discovering it was a dream. Many days and nights, I wondered, How is this my life? That question always smacked of desperation. My first encounter with that question was a blessing.

CHAPTER 21
The Only Way Out Is Through

Having your demons around is quite comforting. Despair is my demon. It covered me like a lead blanket in my prison cell hours after my conviction. As I rebuilt my life, my devil became a shawl over my shoulders. Best days, a ribbon in my hair. It never leaves. In the wrong conditions, before I realize it, it might suffocate me again.

That happened in April 2019, when Chris and I moved into our first house. We were unloading and organizing when the Italy Innocence Project called. This two-person organization, which established after my case, was having its inaugural justice conference and wanted me to speak on "trial by media." The Italian justice minister would attend. The scientific police chief. All of Italy would watch.

I didn't realize it until then, but I was thinking about how to get back to Italy. People thought I would never return to the nation. Even recommending an Italian place for dinner was excused. But I love Italian food and culture. I came to Italy for that. That hadn't altered in four years in Capanne.

Italy and I had unfinished business. Now that returning was possible, I was terrified.

On one hand, I wanted to relate my experience to those who had imprisoned me and still saw me as a criminal person who got off on a technicality or political pull. I couldn't see how I would return (I couldn't just book a ticket and saunter back into the country), but here was an opportunity to speak about one of the main factors that had led to my wrongful conviction. It seemed impossible to find a better chance.

However, I didn't want to keep repeating my worst experience, using my trauma as my only resource that everyone cared about. Most didn't then either. Was my wisdom a figment of my imagination? Was I kidding myself about helping anyone? I was who? Just a girl who was mistreated and would never do anything more than be accused of murder.

My monster spoke. My devil encouraged me to be resentful and alone, ignoring how facing my past may heal others and myself. It wanted me impatient, angry, exploited, and weary. Stop gazing at my wounds—I see up here! It wanted me to think nothing I did mattered.

This invitation was too late for Chris and me to thoroughly organize the trip as the celebration was only two months away. I struggled over the choice and worried about privacy. I had no idea how Italy would treat me. My demon says someone will shiv you on the street. It was hard to ignore that voice when it could be right. Perugia's spectators chanted, "Vergogna! Vergogna!" shame! shame!—after my acquittal. My acquaintance was hit in the face after leaving court. My demon stated the Italian police will arrest you for nonsense. Not impossible again. I was charged with criminal libel for testifying that cops beat me during interrogation. My demon was right. I risked re-arrest by telling my experience.

I asked my friends and family, and they all said don't risk it. No need to go. You can videocall. Record a speech. Why risk it? My lawyers opposed it. They worried about more than police. Could any hotel promise no hidden cameras in our rooms? Can an Airbnb host sell us to paparazzi? Chris was the only one who understood how important this was to me, even though I couldn't express it. My mom didn't understand why I wanted to travel, but she said she'd come if I did. She wouldn't let her daughter visit Italy again alone.

Finally, I said, "Screw it, I have to go." We bought tickets, and while thinking about security and how to avoid being torn apart by the Italian media—which was already frothing at my return—I had to figure out what I was going to say when I stepped onto that stage under the glare of a spotlight with hundreds of cameras and the eyes of Italy and the world watching me.

I had no idea how to start thinking about what to say. I gave presentations, interviews, and essays about my life. I wrote a memoir. I felt like starting over. This chance required a complete reassessment of what happened, what it meant to me, and what I could offer. After sharing your story several times, you realize you rely on the same words to think about something. Those words make you and your listener feel safe and familiar. Storybooks are our homes. Sometimes you must demolish and rebuild your home.

To communicate with the Italian people, I needed the power and confidence that only comes from real vulnerability. Which required emotional labor to find the correct words. I retreated to my most comfortable form, unsure how to begin. Writing letters in prison became my habit. Must have written thousands of letters. Writing "Dear Italy," at the top of my notebook, merely the prospect of chatting to someone sparked my thinking.

Dear Italy,

There have been rare, rare moments in my life when I experience flashes of premonition. The first was November 6, 2007. I was in the interrogation room again, which I didn't know was an interrogation room. I had been yelled at all night, slapped, and told I didn't remember, that I had amnesia, and I tried and tried to remember what I didn't remember, I tried to think of who murdered Meredith. And what did it really mean when my boss Patrick Lumumba texted me that night? And my mind was trying to figure out why I was being pushed and bullied and abused. As my interrogators leapt up and embraced each other for breaking me, as they scattered from the suffocating room, I had a flash of premonition. I was going to suffer. I was going to suffer long and hard. Something was terribly wrong, and I didn't yet know why or how, but I was going to suffer.

When I was stripped naked and photographed by police officers, I was too tired and scared to question them, to object when they examined my genitals for signs of sexual violence. When they put metal handcuffs around my wrists and drove me away in a police car, I believed them when they said it would only be for a few days, that I was an important witness, that I was being taken to a holding place for my own protection. I didn't know. I didn't know that this was just the beginning of my suffering.

I had another flash of premonition when I landed in Seattle for the first time after my imprisonment and I breathed in the fresh, wet, grassy air that I hadn't smelled in years. It came suddenly: I'm going back. I felt it more than I thought it, because I really didn't know if or how I would return to you. I intuitively knew our story was not over.

I reviewed my writing. It's crap, my devil said. Get rid of it. No words are ever right. Why talk? No point. You won't be heard.

The weeks before our departure, Chris and I had a looping conversation about why I was doing this and what I would say. While writing, I discovered that I was describing my own experience, including being fucked over, a twenty-year-old girl who lost a friend, being brutally interrogated, mentally shattered, and thrown in a prison cell. The world labeled her a monster, and she contemplated suicide thousands of miles away. Thinking about that made me angry and sad. But I realized I couldn't just say, "This is how you fucked me over," in Italy. Something had to happen immediately. I had to make this story appealing to a hostile Italian audience. I never tried to prove people wrong on principle since it makes me miserable and unproductive. I knew I was right without telling Italy they were wrong to detain me.

Quite funny. My favorite stories are about gray areas where it's uncertain who's right and wrong. If a seventeen-year-old killer committed the crime before their adult brain evolved, should they be sentenced to life? Should drugs be banned? Overdoses and addiction cost society, but so does the violent and ineffectual war on drugs. Answering them is difficult. It's partly why my predicament has always frustrated me. The Italian courts, media, and public have portrayed it as a byzantine, unclear gray space, while in fact it's a plain, black-and-white story. No one died. I, Raffaele, and Rudy Guede know that. Although the evidence is plain, everyone else must infer the truth. It undoubtedly implicates Guede alone. However, illogical doubts have clouded everything. Why? I had to answer that in my speech.

My speaking developed as we neared our trip, but my demon became stronger and my confidence in leaving weakened. Panic attacks returned. Chris discovered me crying in the closet several times. About to return back where Meredith lost everything and where I lost nearly everything. It was like rafting on a river where you nearly drowned or being raped at a park picnic. My demon says you now have more to lose. I owned a house, was engaged, had friends, was establishing a profession telling important stories, and was healthy, safe, and happy. Why? Why would I return to the place that stole so much?

My monster made me list everything taken in Italy. Even simple things. The cops took most of my stuff and destroyed, lost, or never returned them. I lost my laptop, camping gear, clothes, toiletries, and books. My house, privacy, independence, anonymity, identity, roommate, and time were gone. 1 428 days. Lost family contact. I barely saw my sisters for a few hours every six months. They grew up without me.

To listen to others, I read philosophy books. The stoics wanted me to exorcise my demon. Marcus Aurelius said, "Everything is either endurable or not. If it's bearable, do it. No more whining. If it's unbearable, quit moaning. Your demise will end it." That was fine. I learned a lot from Aurelius, Seneca, and other stoics. It felt wrong to reject my demon this way. Was part of me. Carl Jung may have viewed the shadow as the psyche's blind spot. "The shadow personifies everything that the subject refuses to acknowledge about himself," he wrote. I have self-doubt, worthlessness, and powerlessness. Jung believed that repressing this shadow causes us to subconsciously project it onto our surroundings, altering our perceptions and thoughts. We cannot ignore it. Making it conscious is the goal. Everyone has a shadow, and the less they embody it, the darker and denser it gets. It stymies our best efforts in all ways.

Jung believed you should incorporate your devil or shadow into your conscious self. It's like admitting you're drunk or afraid of commitment. It has many benefits. Jung considered the shadow the "seat of creativity." It hides both our flaws and our promise. The gloom is a small door that cramps everyone who descends to the deep well. You must know yourself to know who you are."

I'm no Jung scholar, so I can't verify all his psychological ideas, yet this resonated. I couldn't conquer my sadness, but I could wear it like a ribbon in my hair, like my semicolon tattoo from a suicide survivor, a symbol for a horrible moment that wasn't an end but a stop. If I could wear my devil that way, it wouldn't distort my environment and would remind me how deep the abyss is and that I should be proud of every inch I climb toward the light.

Chris seeing me fight my demon and understanding I couldn't run helped a lot. He gently reintroduced breathing whenever terror struck. If anyone saw me like that, they would have said, "You don't have to leave. You can cancel tickets now." He never said that. However, he continually asked, "Why are you doing this?"

Even if my answer changed, articulating it helped me center. My mind pictured an unpleasant supper with an ex-lover I hadn't spoken to since the breakup. The relationship and breakup were terrible, but I started dating that person for a reason. My motives for going to Italy were still there.

I turned it to Chris after his hundredth request. "Why are we doing this?" I requested. He paused awhile, then responded, "Because truly beautiful things come from difficult places. This is a chance to create something beautiful."

My life's abyss has frequently felt insurmountable to get out of. It was impossible to prove my innocence to everyone. I couldn't go back to my pre-Italy reputation, anonymity, trauma, killed friend, or those amazing years of being a young lady full of adventure, discovery, and joy. I kept dreaming. If I could cast one spell, lift one pebble with my mind, maybe all those other impossible things would become puzzles—difficult, but at least solveable. Maybe I could turn my devil into a guardian angel. That was what I was doing—learning to recognize its voice as a sign of essential information and my worries to overcome.

Despite all the terrible things I encountered, I kept coming back to one dream. Could I reach the heart of the man who sent me to prison? Could I convince Dr. Giuliano Mignini, whose acts had ruined my life, tarnished my reputation, and brought sadness into my life, to understand me? See my true self? Could I forgive him after letting go of my anger?

These questions were unusual to ask myself because they didn't sound nice or healing. All seemed impossible. No matter, I wrote him a note. To my surprise, it was easier than telling Italy. Just telling him I wanted to see him in person unlocked the remainder of my speech. I returned to Italy not to confront my pain, defend my innocence, or raise awareness about wrongful convictions, but to extend an olive branch to Dr. Giuliano Mignini and the Italian people.

My family was astonished when I informed them I was contacting him. Why on earth would you talk to that monster? After his treatment of our family? His delusions, criminality, and assholery were criticized. While insulting him, I heard them ask me, Amanda, what's wrong? Although I love my family, I recognized their hurt and judgment. If I gave in, I would remain in a grievance prison cell forever. I always wanted to talk to you outside the interrogation room and courtroom, where we were compelled to play prosecutor and defendant. I always thought this prevented us from seeing and understanding each other."

I had no idea if he would answer. Reaching him, however impossible, could change my life and what I could do. It would increase my independence like nothing else. I wouldn't let my freedom be impossible.

CHAPTER 22
In Bocca al Lupo

After the Italy Innocence Project announced its conference and speaker schedule a month before the event, hundreds of interview requests from small podcasts to large publications and prime-time news programs rushed in. I declined them all. I said what I had to in Italy.

We reached Milan two days before the meeting. Drive to Modena took two hours. Since Modena was roughly halfway between Milan, Florence, and Venice, I hoped no one would know where to find me and that I could dodge the paparazzi when I entered the country.

I worried when I noticed the customs agent's expression as he scanned my passport and heard his covert radio message to another agent. Chris and I were surrounded when we departed the airport terminal into the parking lot, but my hosts met us on the other side. I faced dozens of cameras and microphones as Chris and I and the Italy Innocence Project lawyers ran the gauntlet. Questions echoed: "Why did you return?" Feels how? Kercher family? The media rarely portrays its worst tendencies honestly, thus even the most reputable papers call this "Amanda Knox is approached by journalists." The New York Times said Amanda Knox "engaged in a familiar and uneasy tango with the news media." This was not an approach, tango, or voluntary dance or engagement. This was assault. My trauma response began. I walked slowly, head down, as my hosts led me to the car. Hyperventilating began when the door closed. I calmed down after losing the freeway paparazzi. I worried my hosts would underestimate the media problem, and our airport arrival was bad. They underestimated the media's appetite—my return to Italy made headlines worldwide.

Conference attendees had a cocktail hour that night. I declined my hosts' invitation since reporters would be allowed in. "We have to give them something," I was informed. They felt extorted by the mafia. It will get worse if you don't pay protection. They urged me to attend the courtyard cocktail hour if the paparazzi were roped off 30 yards away. I felt like a zoo animal as their telephoto lenses took dozens of photos. I knew they'd pick the most embarrassing photos for the tabloids, and sure enough, my mouth was open wide, mid-laugh, making me look like a cavalier maniac enjoying this trip like one huge party.

Mom met us that night at an Airbnb we reserved in her name as a backup case the Italy Innocence Project's hotel was found. The conference began the next morning, and my address was the next day. I wanted to see other speakers. My exoneree friend Peter Pringle would recount his story. California Innocence Project head Justin Brooks spoke on removing the death penalty. I wanted to help them like they helped me. Chris and I had been hiding in a few back rooms at the conference venue, but we decided to sneak into the auditorium during one talking session. The cameras snapped quickly.

A crowd of journalists was on a circular balcony above us, preparing to cover my speech and looking for me. A flashlight illuminated me in the dark auditorium. Mark Godsey, director of the Ohio Innocence Project, was speaking, but I was the center of attention in the audience. I felt awful for Mark and sensed a panic attack. Chris took me out of the auditorium to the chattering clicks, and I dropped in a stairwell gasping.

After giving me water, one of my hosts gave me a pep talk by holding my shoulders. You're here and nobody expected you. We trust you. We need you. You must fight us because many are like you. You must demonstrate life's continuation. If you flee, many like you will say, 'My life is over, my life is done.' You must assist. Keep your head high. Let them photograph. You stare them in the eye and say "fuck off." She chuckled and said, "But with the eyes, not with words."

She knew I was wondering if anyone wanted me. That was partly because I read too many stories and comments regarding my return to Italy. I was covered by the media before I spoke. Under paparazzi images of me head-bowed in Milan: "She wouldn't keep her head down if she wasn't ashamed." guilty as sin." "She'll do anything for attention."

Reading my trip's commentary seemed like relapsing into a behavior I'd partly overcome. I knew it would depress me, but my optimistic side couldn't resist seeing if someone had anything positive to say.

Instead, I learned that my presence in Italy offended the Kercher family. Piers Morgan tweeted, "Out of respect for Meredith Kercher's poor family, Amanda Knox should stop her self-pitying 'all about me' victim tour—and shut up." He had pushed me to be interviewed on his program before my vacation to Italy, but I declined. Again, the infuriating claim that I was responsible for the media's obsession with me and an attention whore for speaking out about my life's problems in hopes of improving it.

When I arrived in Italy, the Kercher family's lawyer, Francesco Maresca, told the Guardian that my participation in the justice meeting in Modena was "inappropriate" and that I was merely appearing "to keep the attention on [my]self." Never mind that media invited me to speak about trial. Never mind that I had turned down hundreds of interview invitations and would have banished photographers to another realm if I could.

Maresca was constantly rude. "Prison has been good for her," he added of my courtroom gentleness. I'd have been a growling dog if prison had kicked me too many times. I don't blame Kerchers for their lawyer's attitude. They were told a comforting falsehood by the prosecution and their counsel, which the media repeated repeatedly, but Raffaele and I were acquitted, overturning that deception. No bereaved family would find it easy to let go of closure. Maresca told the Guardian what the Kercher family had said since my release: "The murder is a tragic memory for the Kercher family; they lost their daughter and sister in such a terrible way. The fact that they don't know the whole truth is equally unfair.

They implied that Raffaele and I were implicated and unjustly acquitted. All can see the "full truth". But a decade and a half of misinformation had so ingrained the falsehood of a conspiracy, several attackers, and Raffaele and me being involved that they were blind to the truth. Maresca should have focused on Rudy Guede's reduced sentence, which did not adequately account for his actions, if he desired closure. He was never identified as Meredith's killer.

It was frustrating to be accused again of traumatizing the Kercher family by speaking about my wrongful conviction and trying to raise awareness of issues that affect tens of thousands of people. The Innocence Project estimates there are 20,000 to 100,000 innocents in US prisons. We should have been comrades, the Kerchers and I, victims of Rudy Guede and the Italian justice system. I struggled through fear, wrath, and irritation, remembering why I was in Modena. Even on the eve of my talk about media trial, the media continued to outrage and clickbait, distorting my character, imprisoning me in a false narrative years after my acquittal, and overshadowing Meredith's victimhood.

Mom observed my stress and asked me to turn back and go home. "I can book a ticket now," she added. It's not worth it." Love my mom, but I knew she was wrong. I could not give up and travel home early. I had something to say, but much more important was that I was willing to say it here, in front of a potentially hostile crowd. For once, people may listen. This challenged my bravery. I reached the top of the tallest diving board. Standing on the edge. If fear of condemnation makes me crawl back down that ladder, I might as well be in prison. Something stronger than me would decide and guide my life. Even though I knew this and felt more determined, I was an emotional disaster and scared about my safety.

The Italy Innocence Project sent a former special forces carabinieri officer as my Modena private security guard. I distrust Italian cops, but he shocked me. He took us to a tiny agriturismo an hour outside town for dinner with the other conference presenters the night before my session. Agriturismos, vacation rentals on antique or still-operating farms, are prevalent in rural Italy. It was the only way to evade paparazzi. We'd be back in the car flying away by the time someone spotted me out there and told journalists. This Italian military police officer recited Dante on dark, twisting roads into the countryside, and Chris offered him Robert Frost, Borges, and an Italian poetry he'd memorized by Eugenio Montale in English, Spanish, and Italian. I felt his genuine kindness and hoped I could reach the Italian people in my address the next day.

Before we went into the countryside, I felt like I was fighting an impossible struggle. As usual, the press was harsh. None of the articles by the hour noted that I was invited to speak, that I was raising awareness of justice system issues, and that I wasn't compensated. The Italy Innocence Project, whose phone was ringing nonstop, was repeating these talking points, but they didn't fit the notion that I was exploiting Meredith's misfortune for attention. I felt more confined in this tale than in a while.

But that dinner at the agriturismo was just what I needed: a beautiful evening in the country overlooking olive orchards, a family-style meal with friends, decanters of wine, homemade amaro, and bats chasing insects in the twilight. It was exactly what I came to Italy for—a classic Italian experience. I believed I'd never return to Italy, yet there it was—food, warmth, wine, camaraderie.

As we tried to fall asleep, Chris asked me what I would tell my younger self about this time. It hit me immediately: "I know it doesn't feel this way, but everything doesn't depend on whether or not people believe you, because the people who matter do." Not everyone has Chris, my mom, and my family. I was lucky. A part of me believed that my Italy experience defined me forever. I knew I was more than the worst event of my life no matter what happened the next day. Italy allowed me to act and restore agency.

That moment brought me peace, if not with the world. My inner angst from months before this vacation was gone. I knew I was doing my best and pushed myself. I knew I was done. Masochism—an inability to love and accept myself until I gave everything—was also at play. I didn't know how to change that relationship, but I knew I had it in me to stand on that stage, more vulnerable than I had been in a while, and tell the Italian people and the world the truth.

I wasn't sure how Italy would react to my message. I stopped caring about being crucified or applauded. The gates of hell in Dante's Inferno say, "Abandon All Hope Ye Who Enter Here." I always assumed that meant hell is a place of agony with no escape. Paradoxically, it's survival counsel. Hope, like fear, ignores the present and lives in the future. It prevents you from appreciating your home, employment, and early spring sun. In prison, it hindered me from accepting my situation, and in freedom, it kept me in a destructive relationship. I had to give up hope. I couldn't endure without hope, without any idea of how my speech would be received or its impact. Without hope, I was unstoppable.

CHAPTER 23
Coraggio

I woke up quiet and solemn after a restful sleep. I had trouble imagining following the speech. I could hardly imagine performing. My imagination built a wall before the podium. I read that courage is mastery over dread, the belief that something else is more important than fear, from Nelson Mandela to Mark Twain. That wall in my mind prevented me from imagining how people would react to my speech, which was my greatest fear—that I'd open my heart and be booed, have things thrown at me, be attacked, or, more realistically but more crushingly, be dismissed, remain unheard, and have tabloids twist my words to confirm the time-tested, money-generating narrative: Amanda Knox = Bad. As the lawyer who introduced me went on and on, explaining to the audience and press why they had invited me and why my presence was fitting and important at a criminal justice reform conference, I realized that even my hosts were worried.

Finally, my name was called. The crowd was silent as I neared the podium. The jumbotron screen showed my face twenty feet tall. I drank water, breathed deeply, and spoke Italian:

This is my third trip to Italy. I came here when I was fourteen. My whole extended family piled into minivans and toured the Colosseum and the ruins of Pompeii. We ate snails on the Amalfi coast. I fell in love with Italy on that trip. And when I returned as a twenty-year-old, to write poetry, drink wine, and take siestas, I was met instead with tragedy and suffering. Despite that, or because of it, Italy became a part of me. Language and culture shaped my mind. I have returned a third time because I have to, because I've been invited by the Italy Innocence Project, and because this beautiful country once felt like home to me, and I hope that it will feel that way again.

A lot of people think I'm crazy to return. I've been told it's unsafe. That I'll be attacked in the streets. That I'll be falsely accused and sent back to prison. That even if I return home unscathed, it will all be for nothing.

Frankly, I'm afraid. I'm afraid of being harassed. I'm afraid of being mocked. I'm afraid of being framed. I'm afraid new charges will be brought against me just for telling the truth here today. But most of all, I'm afraid my courage will fail me.

I know that despite my acquittals by the Court of Cassation, I remain a controversial figure in the court of public opinion, especially here in Italy. I know many people think I'm a villain. That I don't belong here. Some have even claimed that just by being here, I am re-traumatizing the Kercher family, and desecrating Meredith's memory.

They are wrong. And the fact that I continue to be held accountable in this way—for the Kerchers' grief, for Perugia's reputation—shows how powerful false narratives can be and how they can undermine justice, especially when they are reinforced and amplified by the media. But the media can also reveal and amplify the truth, if journalists are brave enough to see it, and if the public demands it.

My voice was shaking, but I pushed through, telling the audience the tragic details of what had actually happened to Meredith, how we knew this with certainty from the evidence, and how attention came to focus on me instead of Rudy Guede. I broke down recounting my interrogation and the forced admission I signed after being gaslit by authority persons for hours late at night. The event was key to understanding why the Perugia police reported "case closed" after detaining Patrick, Raffaele, and me before lab results arrived. I continued:

This was a hasty and unfounded conclusion, a grave mistake. And this was the moment the media could have shined. Because the media is our first line of defense to hold our authorities accountable, especially when they wield their power to strip us of our freedom. It was here that journalists could have asked, "You've charged and arrested three people. Based on what evidence? You say the American girl confessed. Are her statements legally sound, coherent, reliable, and do they correspond with the evidence?" In so doing, the media could have incentivized the police to slam the brakes on an investigation that was veering wildly and blindly off the road.

Instead, the media pumped the gas. Without incriminating physical evidence, the police attacked my character, distorting my rather normal sexual history into deviancy so I'd fit into their "sex game gone wrong" theory. The media took this and ran with it.

On the world stage, I wasn't a defendant—innocent until proven guilty. I was a liar, a psychopath, a dirty, drug-addled slut so jealous of Meredith's purity that I raped and killed her—guilty until proven innocent. It was a false and unfounded story, but it sparked the world's imagination. It spoke to people's fears and fantasies.

This cycled back into the courtroom, polluting the jury pool and any chance of a fair trial. I took the audience inside prison to feel that guilty verdict. I told them about my friendship with Don Saulo, who never judged me or told me who I was, even while the world dubbed me a monster. I told them he helped me develop a mindset of compassion, understanding, and thankfulness, which helped me understand what occurred to me.

It's not enough to get it right eventually. We need to get it right sooner, far more often than we do. And the media can be a powerful force in helping us do that. In those four years of prison, eight years of trial, and to this day, I have borne many costs for the mistakes of others. I want to share them with you, not to garner your pity, but to show you what happens when we get it wrong, in the hope that the next innocent person on trial suffers far less than I have.

I told them of my thoughts of suicide, the impact on my family, and I broke down in tears when I spoke about a time my father came to visit.

My family was only allowed to visit me for six hours a month. Once, my dad came, and I just couldn't hold it together. I was so tired of fear and uncertainty, loss and loneliness. I couldn't help it. I just started sobbing. And my dad held me. And I pleaded with him. I begged him to save me, even though I knew he was just as helpless as I was. And my dad had to tell me what my lawyers had told him: that it would likely be several years before I could expect another serious chance at freedom. And then he started crying. All he could do was cry with me. And that's when I knew how bad it was, because I had never seen my father cry before in my entire life.

These costs weren't mine. Not necessary or inevitable. I argued the legal system and media are instruments, not good or bad, but only as just as their users. Our courtrooms are often battlegrounds where the most engaging story triumphs, not the most factual. Media increased the battlefield devastation in my case. The reverse may have happened.

Finally, I discussed my prosecutor. I knew this moment would be controversial and that my family wouldn't like what I said.

Recently, I've been thinking a lot about my prosecutor, Dr. Giuliano Mignini. For a long time, I've hoped for the chance to meet face-to-

face with him outside the interrogation room and courtroom, where we were forced into the adversarial roles ascribed to us—prosecutor and defendant, good and evil. I've always suspected that this, perhaps above all, made it impossible for us to understand each other. Because to my twenty-year-old self, wrongly imprisoned and on trial, Dr. Giuliano Mignini was a nightmarish figure—a powerful and frightening man who had only one goal: to destroy my life.

I know that image of him is wrong. It is as flat and two-dimensional as Foxy Knoxy. It was the media that helped me see that. In the Netflix documentary, I saw not an evil man, but a man with genuine, noble motivations, who wanted to bring justice to a grieving family. I would like to meet that man, the real Dr. Giuliano Mignini, one day. And I hope that when that time comes, he, too, can come to see that I am not a monster, but that I am simply Amanda.

I have the same hope in being here with you all today. That by having the courage to stand before you, and meet with you face-to-face, we can arrive at some kind of understanding and reconciliation between us. Because true justice happens when we see our fellow human beings with compassion, when we judge with restraint, and when we return to each other, after pain and enmity, with the courage of an open heart.

I thanked them and mentioned the innocence movement and my exoneree family. Two unexpected events followed. Standing ovation from the crowd. My Italian speech startled them, and they listened closely for an hour. My hosts expected me to speak English, but I came to Italy to connect with the Italian people in their language. No one booed. No tomato was thrown at me. Instead, I received thunderous cheers. I was still astonished when the security man off to the side led me backstage, away from the crowd, down a twisting hallway to the basement, where I would be safe. He grasped my shoulders, looked me in the eyes, and murmured, "Perfetto." Perfect. I sobbed into his shoulder while hugging him.

I didn't talk to the audience, but hundreds of Italians gave me comments through the hostesses. Reading these messages, some of which apologized for judging me, made me cry again.

Chris and I dropped Mom off at Milan airport the next morning and drove to the northern border in our rented car. We scheduled a few days on the south coast of France to relax. I saw the email in my inbox from a historic hilltop village overlooking the Mediterranean. It came from my prosecutor, Dr. Giuliano Mignini. I sent him two letters in recent months through Don Saulo and a reliable Italian journalist. He refused to read them, I was told. He considered it improper. He wrote me back. After hearing my speech, he had to answer.

CHAPTER 24
Dear Giuliano

After returning from Modena and calming down, I began talking to my prosecutor in early August 2019. Why would you want to talk to this man who framed you as a sex-crazed killer, imprisoned you for four years, and tried you for eight? One answer: I wondered why. Why did this happen to me? Why did he think I deserved it? Why couldn't I let go? I kept thinking about those questions. If speaking at the Italy Innocence Project event was brave, seeking this dialogue was curious.

I knew judgment hindered real curiosity. When we don't judge, we may perceive reality more clearly. We consider people flawed and complicated. Seeing this also weakens our judges. If I thought Dr. Giuliano Mignini was nasty and corrupt, like most of my family, friends, and supporters, I would learn nothing. His prosecution of the wrong individuals made me a cartoon villain for the world to judge. I knew people were incorrect about me, and I didn't want to be wrong about anyone else. Especially him. That impulse was rebellious and contrarian, rejecting my victimhood. If I did what everyone expected—fear and shun him—I was still a product of his mistakes. But if I did what everyone least expected, I shaped my own future.

It felt noble and infantile, like a teenager quitting the family company to play Ping-Pong. Mutinies enrich the world. In a world of constant judgment, inquiry and compassion were my revolt. Avoiding judgment was my habit. Radical empathy or extreme benefit of doubt.

Giuliano wrote to me long in his first letter, using the informal "tu" form like I did. Through media tragedy, he and I connected. The press also misinterpreted his character and deeds. My remarks, especially regarding my father's visit, a decent guy who suffered in silence, affected him. But he said he had done nothing wrong, had never been hostile toward me, and was only doing his job. He ended by calling me "a happy surprise."

It took me over a month to reply. It was hard to believe I was talking to this man. Naturally, I wrote him back in Italian, saying, "Part of me is relieved to know that you never felt hostility toward me and that you never considered me a monster. Part of me despairs that there is no simple explanation for why you detected guilt in me that wasn't there." I told him about my brutal police interrogation, that I planned to appeal my slander conviction for the statements I was pressured to sign, and that I hoped we would meet in court again as allies in the service of the truth. I also asked to meet face-to-face, privately, without media.

Two months passed before he responded. His letters kept appearing in my hectic life like frightening oncologist messages: Your findings are in. Call me to discuss. I would go from work or Christmas planning to Trauma Land. Mignini's words ached to read, yet I couldn't leave them alone for more than a minute.

His letters startled me with their need for connection. He said I helped him reconnect with Don Saulo, his parish priest and longtime buddy. As time smooths their sharp corners, he spoke longingly like many aging men. He said he regularly looked at trial images, especially ones of us together. He noticed my painful looks and my sorrowful gaze, as if I wanted to converse. He was right.

The Court of Cassation's final verdict still bothered him. He still cared about "procedural matters," furious that they hadn't followed precedent and remanded the case to a lesser appeals court instead of acquitting Raffaele and me. He told me that our acquittal had sparked a wave of attacks on him in Italy, and that his beloved dog Arlo, who had blue eyes like mine, died in his arms.

It's hard to get mad with a man holding his dying dog. Perhaps he knew. But I also recognized it must be hard to be furious at a fearful girl screaming for her mother in a cell. I explained the rules and purpose of our correspondence: See the other's humanity. He tried hard. He was honest with me about what bothered him about the past: how the police interrogated me, even though he only came in at the end, and how the police chief's "case closed" comment was attributed to him, even though he called out his colleague for making such a mistake. He even speculated that my original interview would have gone differently if he had been there.

He still spoke of his role in the inquiry and trials in lofty terms of logic and deduction. "The investigator must reconstruct a past event which he did not observe," he wrote, "a bit like a historian." A good investigator needs curiosity, intelligence, attention to detail, complete lack of preconceptions and training, logical rigor, and profound humility to find the truth. He must follow his hypothesis, but he must be ready to reassess it if his 'assumption' is arbitrary and unproven."

Cognitive dissonance dropped my jaw. He wild-guessed that I was "morbidly obsessed with violence and sex" and had planned an orgy-turned-murder with a young man I barely knew. He considered himself unbiased, reasonable, humble, and willing to challenge his beliefs.

He said something more in his letter that shocked me even more. In his writing, he acknowledged the possibility of mistakes and the distinction between official and real truths. Make sure the two truths match. This touches me as much as you do." According to the decision, you were all present, but Meredith's murderer cannot be determined. The guilty party could have been one individual, or anything else. It is possible that the judges made a mistake, but we cannot change it. The verdict is final."

He was accepting the possibility that he could have been wrong, not fault? Could Rudy Guede have acted alone? He spoke so carefully that I wondered if he worried legal repercussions for himself or his office. The verdict from the Court of Cassation, which acquitted me and Raffaele, incorrectly claimed we were there at the crime scene that night, even though we were not involved in the murder. They did so because they believed unreliable confession evidence: if I signed a statement indicating I was at the house that night, it meant I was. Even the smart judges who acquitted us were unaware of forceful interrogations and phony admissions.

That twisted knot of sentiment was even harder to understand when he signed off with, "Merry Christmas from your prosecutor." I realized when I got outraged that I hadn't expected him to apologize, accept responsibility, or beg pardon. I had to be content with following this correspondence. I learnt from my Modena trip that letting go of a desired objective sometimes lead to unexpected, although challenging, blessings. Giuliano and I exchanged holiday greetings on December 25 and January 1. In this brief period, he had become a kind, distant uncle.

After the epidemic, I wrote him back to apologize for the three-month delay and explain how confused and anxious I felt when I noticed his email in my inbox. That was partly because I knew he still didn't believe I was innocent. "I don't think I will ever feel at peace," I wrote, "even though I work every day to resign myself to the fact that I can never convince you and all the other people in the world that I was tried and imprisoned as an innocent person But I also told him how precious this dialogue was to me and how it gave me courage and comfort to share even tiny understandings with him—what it feels like to be misrepresented and mistreated by the media—even if we still had major and life-changing misunderstandings.

His response came a week later. Despite blaming the cops and calling himself "gruff," he stated he loved individuals he trusted. Yes, I did. He was really moved by my outreach. "I will never forget the grandness of your soul," he wrote. He loved Wagner and Lord of the Rings: "I am a 'chivalrous' Catholic, like King Theoden of Rohan. You resemble Eowyn." He claimed our correspondence made him feel like we understood each other like few do. Although I was hesitant, I wanted a real relationship, especially when he said, "I'm happy for you." Could he be glad I was free? "I tried to do my duty," he wrote, "and I may have made a mistake." He returned to this delicate near-apology. When he did, I longed for him to believe in my innocence and take responsibility for his faults. I initiated this conversation but couldn't stop it. I could only react thoughtfully and attempt to see what was happening between us without being blinded by my desires. He later wrote, "It does not seem to me that I led those journalists in portraying you so differently from how you are, but if it happened, I ask your forgiveness." He declared, "Today, I defend you always and everywhere."

Honestly, I was stunned. I would have known if he was continually protecting me. International headlines would have read, "Italian Prosecutor Admits to Making Mistakes, Amanda Knox Is Innocent." Another part of me watched him struggling to get there, so close to accepting responsibility. He must be struggling, I understood. He was defined by his integrity. He had to concede that, despite great intentions, he had committed a huge mistake that had deprived Meredith's family of closure and hurt Raffaele and myself. He'd have to see himself as someone who had distorted justice rather than restoring it.

He recommended Una Vita in Gioco (A Life on the Line), an Italian detective film based on a French novel about Inspector Maigret, at the end of his letter. He promised that this film would show the investigator's suffering after a trial, which he felt for me.

With the pandemic, he advised we keep in touch before meeting in person. He ended with "A hug, Giuliano."

Hugs from my prosecutor? I'd gotten into what?

CHAPTER 25
A New Life

I envisioned being a mother since childhood. Having kids was a given. I could be released into free society at 46 after my guilty verdict. My freedom and motherhood would likely be taken if that happened. I didn't know who I was at that point, but I knew I wasn't the media's girl and that I was a nurturer, caregiver, and mom-in-waiting. Looking at my mom, who loved my sister and me, I wanted to be like her. Where would I pour my love? Not into my kid, but into an empty future.

I was twenty-eight when I was acquitted and allowed to dream about beginning a family. It could have been lot worse. I met other unfortunate ladies through the Innocence Network. My friend was sentenced to life and served almost fifteen years before being exonerated. The end of her fertility window came, and she quit up after many fertility treatments, failed implantations, and a miscarriage.

This is rarely addressed in prisons for women. Long and severe sentences kill both men and women's productive years, but men's reproductive functions don't. Women who receive extended sentences are sentenced to infertility and time.

I felt lucky to think about having kids with Chris while considering all of this. Now that I could be a mother, I had no time to waste! I didn't want to share that adventure with Giuliano because he nearly took it from me.

At 25, my mother gave birth to me. She struggled as a single mom teaching elementary school after being divorced when I was one year old and pregnant with my sister Deanna. She joked about fixing the trauma by making me pledge at seven that I wouldn't become pregnant until thirty. I signed a green crayon contract we made.

Once I was out of legal trouble at 25, she asked, "Where's my grandbabies?" I was ready when Chris and I got engaged at thirty-one, but Chris wanted to wait until after we were married. I visited Planned Parenthood a few weeks into the pandemic, excited to tell the women who had helped me prevent unwanted pregnancy for years, "You know how you're called Planned Parenthood? I'm planning that crap."

As they removed the IUD, it broke in half, so I had to see a specialist again to remove the rest. I don't believe in omens, therefore it didn't bother me. The full-blown outbreak worried me and Chris. The grocery store ran out of toilet paper, and society seemed more fragile than ever. The cancellation of public events wiped off our income overnight, and we worried about defaulting on our mortgage. Is it time to have a child? There's no right time, they say.

I started talking to my baby and making films for them when we started trying to conceive. It was wonderful to imagine their embarrassment. After our first effort, we filmed my butt on a pillow. For my future child, I told the camera, "Hope you exist soon!" After years of having my life chronicled by judging lenses without my agreement, filming these funny videos for our new family was liberating.

A positive pregnancy test was predictable and joyful. Chris and I, keen planners, started decorating the baby room straight early, painting a colorful mural on the wall and choosing our cot and changing table. Only weeks had passed! We heard the advice to wait a few months to tell people, but Mother's Day was approaching, and we wanted to surprise our moms. I cross-stitched a beautiful fetus and prepared framed gifts for my mom, stepmom, and Chris's mom. They squealed with delight.

Chris waited outside by the elevators and Zoomed into the first ultrasound appointment without me due to COVID rules. I really wanted him to hear the heartbeat on the phone. I shone at that eight-week ultrasound despite COVID-19 and being apart from my husband. After all my misfortunes, something was right.

The technician inquired, "When was your last period?" while I was in the stirrups and a wand probing my body. Are you sure about timing? She couldn't hear heartbeat. "It's looking like you're early," she remarked. "Maybe you counted wrong."

The fetus was six weeks, not eight. They invited me back in a week to try again. Chris believed we had miscounted, but I had a strong suspicion that something was amiss and that the technician didn't want to inform me.

Deanna, my sister who had fertility issues, remarked, "Oh." when I informed her about the appointment. She said nothing more but suggested we talk after my next checkup. I felt like I had found a secret club no one would admit existed. I was upset, and as that week went on, I became increasingly convinced that the medical professionals and my sister were hiding information from me until it was my turn to know. When I went on trial, my lawyers were more upfront about my fate.

The fetus hadn't grown and there was no heartbeat when we returned to the ultrasound room. How might I interpret that news? Why did my body not understand the fetus was dead? I'd never heard of missed miscarriage. I believed bleeding would indicate a miscarriage. I was pregnant with a baby that had stopped growing. This news left me numb, not crying. "Your body will probably figure it out sooner or later," the doctor remarked, "but it could take weeks." Weeks? I hated the idea, so she gave me drugs to empty my womb.

I stumbled to the drugstore counter when we stopped. After reading my prescription, the pharmacist glanced at me and said, "I'm sorry." I quietly sobbed and said, "Thanks," my speech limited to one-word sentences. "Have you done this before?" she inquired. Shaking my head no. I nodded calmly as she explained.

I didn't talk to Chris in the car. We drove with him holding my hand. We visited my mom's house before going home and found her in the backyard conversing with Chris's mom, who had returned some Tupperware. I gave them those cute fetus cross-stitches on Mother's Day, exposing our pregnancy early despite knowing something may happen. Chris and I decided it was okay to inform some individuals we could grieve with if something horrible happened. Some part of me wanted to do that when my joyful mom asked, "How'd it go!?" Though both moms smiled at me, I just shook my head. Chris's mother said, "Oh," crying. I knew they wanted to hug me, but I couldn't stand it. I felt silly, not for telling them, but for believing I deserved a win here, that after all that had gone wrong and Dr. Giuliano Mignini and others had hurt me, I needed this most crucial thing to go right. I fooled who? It was my fate to endure. Chris followed me to the car when I turned left.

I had already addressed my stomach. I was mentally using our male and girl names. The pregnancy app showed her as big as a kiwi and her skin forming each week. That ultrasound image of a dying fetus stuck in my head as we pulled into the driveway, and I kept telling myself: That wasn't my baby. There was no name.

I waited on the bed after taking the medications. After an hour, I felt acute abdominal cramps for the first time. Shaking and crushed. Chris cuddled me to keep me warm and convinced me to take the doctor's pain medication, which I had refused. Thirty minutes later, it halted the trembling. This encounter leaves me with more than physical pain. Long, recurring quiet in the bathroom as I produced blood wads over two days. The largest clump was plum-sized. I peered in the toilet every time a fresh clump came out, wondering, Is that my baby? Is that it?

I thought my body betrayed me. My nervousness rose and I wondered: Is this the start? Do I have rotten eggs? Too old? Did prison trauma—malnutrition, weight loss, and poor medical care—affect my fertility?

Giuliano kept writing me, sending many letters for every one I returned, and he said something that upset me: "Excuse me if I say so, but I know I can speak openly with you. Have you considered motherhood? It would be great to know there is another 'Amanda' besides my beloved."

CHAPTER 26
Una Vita in Gioco

Without being pregnant and looking for distractions, I found a blurry clip of Giuliano's Italian detective film on YouTube. Inspector Maigret arrests and convicts Huertin of double homicide in the film. Death sentence for Huertin. Maigret doubts Huertin's guilt and believes he prosecuted the wrong person. He convinces a judge to release the condemned. Maigret then follows Huertin to discover who he interacts with, finding the proof he needs to arrest Radek, the genuine killer, and liberate Heurtin.

I was stunned again. This account showed Mignini's anguish over the case that characterized his career and unjustly derailed my life? I couldn't believe it.

Mignini connected with Maigret. The likeness is uncanny. They are huge, respected men who dress simply but professionally. Both smoke pipes. They both have morals that sometimes get them in trouble with authorities. Both consider themselves Sherlock Holmes-like detectives who use circumstantial evidence to solve problems. A, B, C are logical deductions that necessarily lead to the truth.

Did Mignini regard me as Huertin, the falsely accused, or Radek, the killer, if he saw himself as Maigret?

Innocent Heurtin is on execution row neither because Maigret, who investigated him, or the judge who presided over his trial made any mistakes. Since the process was meticulous, the judge thinks Maigret is foolish to doubt and accuses him of being irrationally "in love with the idea of Heurtin's innocence." However, Maigret concedes that some aspects of the case are unclear, some facts don't fit, and some evidence may have only "imagined significance." To find all the facts and their meaning, he must use innovative means.

A typical example of dietrologia, the Italian belief that hidden truths lurk under the surface, that official explanations are rarely accurate, and that things are more than they seem. Radek, the suspicious young foreigner, is still a mystery in the murders. Maigret and Radek play cat-and-mouse in Una Vita in Gioco.

One scene left me breathless. Maigret reflects in a taxi back:

Quando si sente di girare intorno una soluzione, e non si può afferrarla, si è veramente tentato di inventare, di costruire un colpevole. Ma nel momento in cui si riaprono gli occhi ai dati reali, diventano dati erronei.

In English:

When you feel an answer swirling around, and you can't grasp it, you're truly tempted to invent one, to create a culprit. But the moment you open your eyes to the real facts, they become erroneous.

Is Mignini's tacit admission of guilt the closest I've ever received?

I responded after a month of thinking. I started by writing about my family, cats, pandemic isolation, and how not being able to enjoy holidays with my family reminded me of prison. I omitted the miscarriage. I avoided trial research. His kind attitude moved me, and "it makes me feel like the long nightmare is beginning to fade." Finally, I quoted Maigret's statement in the taxicab, expecting he would elaborate.

He gave me Una Vita in Gioco to reveal his case-related anguish. I let him into my world by suggesting he watch "Darmok" from Star Trek: The Next Generation. The episode shows commander Picard trying to interact with a hostile alien commander whose language he can't speak. However, the "enemy" commander forces them to work together to fight an invisible beast on a rocky planet, leading to their cooperation and understanding.

Media misinformation was our common enemy. I only said, "I think humans are less rational than we think we are." I suppose instincts drive us, and our exceptional reasoning talents are largely utilized to justify our preset opinions, not to challenge them."

I sent, "A hug, Amanda," to the man who had imprisoned me for four years and would have kept me in Capanne for the rest of my life.

His next letter reminded me how much he appreciated my acquaintance and how he, his wife, their four daughters, and his kitty, Guli, were surviving the pandemic. He mentioned Maigret again, stating he liked him for his intellectual honesty and that Maigret eventually realized things were not as he imagined.

I thought Giuliano was avoiding "sorry," but he couldn't confess responsibility. I didn't urge him to apologize since I knew I couldn't make him. It was his call. I could only try to see him and have an honest conversation. "I acted in full honesty, believe me," he wrote. Sure, I could have been mistaken. Besides, I didn't know you. Now I know you. Day after day, your qualities impress me."

He informed me Maigret trusted his intuition and followed it. I can tell if someone is honest, good, bad, sincere, or dishonest right away. I trust first impressions, especially body language." He saw a virtue, I saw a major defect.

The gut reaction that made him distrust me was wrong. He and the police may have misinterpreted my conduct and testimony in the early days of the investigation due to cultural differences, conspiratorial thinking, or several lost-in-translation instances. He sought facts to support his first perception, a classic form of confirmation bias. Only unreliable, circumstantial evidence was found. My lawyers always contended that zero plus zero plus zero equaled zero. But Giuliano never saw data to contradict his early intuition. I knew discussing the evidence would never change that. He reached his conclusions without reasoning, thus logic couldn't change them. Instead, my friendship had moved him and changed his intuitions.

Maigret studied Heurtin, not the evidence, to believe he was innocent. Even though Heurtin was at the murder scene, Maigret wondered, "Could this man have committed this crime?" Was he capable?" This was how Mignini perceived me after knowing me through "this growing affection that unites us."

As the pandemic continued, I heard Giuliano's father represented convicts. The women's prison was across the street from Giuliano's childhood home, and he could view the courtyard where female detainees had yard time from his living room. After his father died in a vehicle accident when Giuliano was four, his mother struggled to raise the family. The inmates, who loved his father, gave her their condolences. Inmates who were mothers committed their children to her, and young Giuliano celebrated his birthday with them.

I didn't expect him to have such a profound connection with the inmates, and it was hard to reconcile this with the fact that he'd wanted to send me there for the rest of my life, knowing the true agony prisoners endure. In his prosecution of me, he sincerely believed that I was a dangerous person who should be in prison, however incorrect he was.

He talked about his kitties and that he loved rain and gloomy, snowy days. These letters, on both sides, were full of little things like this—the commonplace but real stuff of real friendships. Trading pleasantries and getting to know each other was as bizarre as his comments on the case and his "mistakes could have been made" assessment of my innocence.

He reaffirmed that he didn't know me before but did now, "thanks to that outstretched hand of your first letter." For me, that begged the inevitable question: why didn't he care to know me when he was spreading lies about me and my motives? His indifference to the dissonance was astounding.

Though frustrating, the need for connection and forgiveness exceeded it. Talking to him was like thrift-shopping. Any Goodwill shopper hoping for a yellow sundress was likely to be disappointed. Being open to finding something wonderful beyond your search—like a mushroom-shaped lamp—made thrifting successful. I found a man unlike the courtroom's stubborn opponent. He stated, "I would like the people of Seattle to know me for who I am after the hostility they showed me at the trial. The name Amanda is lucky. Never forget. A good name. Meaning loving. The name is difficult." He probably meant it was a tall goal to achieve by "challenging". Then he was right. My mom's early admonition to be compassionate helped me live up to my name, yet millions of people still felt I was a monster unworthy of love and hatred.

"I never felt above judgment," I wrote. That's why I looked to you during the trial with grief, not hatred or rage. Without knowing why, I assumed you disliked me. I wanted my true self judged."

He gave me a photo of a rainbow in front of his terrace in early December 2020 as a message of hope. Prisoner Rudy Guede was released the following day.

CHAPTER 27
Rudy Goes Free

On December 6, 2020, the New York Post headlined, "Man Who Killed Amanda Knox's Roommate Freed on Community Service." It did not name Meredith or Rudy Guede, her killer. As usual, it named the footnote-worthy me. Even though I had accepted that Meredith's death was my fate, the way this news was framed nevertheless got to me, and I felt rage erupting.

Ivory Coast-born Rudy Guede. His father took him to Italy at five and abandoned him. His charisma helped him survive several foster homes before he was adopted by a wealthy Peruvian family. After constantly stealing from them, that family disowned him as a teenager. At twenty-one, he was losing control. The month-long burglary spree culminated with Guede's rape and murder of Meredith. He was arrested in Milan for burglarizing a nursery school days before the murder and carrying a weapon. After killing Meredith, he escaped Italy to Germany. The absence of evidence incriminating other suspects and Guede's undeniable guilt were astounding. After telling a confidant, unknowing that police were listening, that I had nothing to do with the crime, he revised his story. He accused me at every chance, following the prosecution and media, and I assumed he would continue to do so after his release. It was difficult for me to believe Guede would confess his misdeeds in freedom. Guede should have been charged, convicted, and sentenced for aggravated rape and second-degree murder in the US, where the federal statutory minimum is life without parole. Guede was convicted and jailed for sexual assault and murder conspiracy in Italy. On appeal, his term was reduced to sixteen years. After 10, he was released for the day. He might finish his sentence in freedom after thirteen years. His crimes were not under Guede's name. I sat in wrath all day, avoiding social media and dismissing media demands for comment. I gained clarity via journaling, meditating, and talking to Chris. I wasn't upset Rudy Guede was free. I wasn't even offended that journalists who kept attacking me were humanizing him by quoting his lawyers, who said he was "calm and socially well-integrated." I wasn't upset about his second opportunity. I think everyone is better than their biggest mistake. Even Rudy Guede deserved another opportunity. However, I was upset. Guede made many people suffer. He created a constellation of anguish for Meredith's family, me, Raffaele, our families, and those who tried to clear our identities. I didn't need to know his thoughts that night, but I wanted to know if he cared about Meredith and me.

After his release, many began questioning, "What should his punishment have been?" Thought about my fellow exonerees. Like Guede, they are mostly guys of color. My friend Juan Rivera was wrongfully convicted of rape and murder and condemned to life. Twenty years served before exoneration. A murder my friend Greg Mingo didn't commit got him life in jail. After forty years, he was pardoned. The average period wrongfully convicted Americans serve before being exonerated is fourteen years, longer than Guede spent in prison for raping and killing someone. Should he have served life? I had thought a lot about punishment and sentencing over the years and seen that both guilty and innocent people are given harsh sentences to serve in places that don't rehabilitate them. Such thoughts constantly took me back to the Golden Rule: "Do unto others as you would have them do unto you." Nearly every major religion promotes reciprocity. Confucius said, "What you do not wish for yourself, do not do to others." I prefer to think of it as setting standards. Treating them as awful as you think they are rarely surprises you, but treating them as excellent as you hope they can be helps them grow. That was my strategy with Giuliano, and he surprised me. I attempted to apply that thinking to the individual who killed my friend and accused me, but it was hard.

My opinions were expressed in an essay rather than in the media. It ended:

I would not wish an unreasonably harsh sentence on anyone. I would wish them only true rehabilitation. Guede's lawyers say he's on that path. Maybe so. But I do know one thing: so long as he refuses to admit his crimes, to show true regret, I will continue to unjustly bear his infamy, be held accountable for the Kerchers' grief, be shamed for not showing remorse for Guede's crime. He could end all that in a second. I doubt he ever will, but the day he does, I will celebrate his rehabilitation and wish him the best on a new and honest chapter of his life.

Giuliano answered my essay on Christmas Eve. He also regretted Guede's short punishment, but he highlighted that he may request a fast-track trial. He didn't like the statute that allowed this process, which decreased major crime punishments, but he had to follow Italian law.

He said Merry Christmas and Happy New Year.

CHAPTER 28
An Uncertain Miracle

Danny's release news buried our correspondence in the trial. Giuliano's adherence to the legal narrative and defense of his actions upset me. "What I did as a prosecutor is over and no one can take it back," he wrote. At the same time, we cannot remove our love. You ask what I would do today if the trial continued. Our relationship made me abstain.

It drove me crazy! He would remark something unexpected, yet continue, "You cannot think that twenty or more judges found you guilty without a reason, based on nothing. They may have been wrong, but you can't try someone without evidence!"

Naturally, he did it. He understood how much talking about the trial hurt me and didn't want me to suffer. "My task today is difficult. This is like removing a thorn from your foot, he wrote.

The more I grasped his opinions and how he reached them, the more I could understand why this injustice had befallen me and the less these debates would hurt me. Till we met, I agreed with him that we shouldn't get into our case disagreements.

After a year of the pandemic, Giuliano sent me loving wishes on my wedding anniversary and Easter. He said he was writing a book about the case to "reveal the real Amanda." I was excited but hesitant about our relationship, just like my parenthood experience.

After my miscarriage, I wanted to get back on track, but my period hadn't returned for months. When it did, negative tests followed. Chris and I had rabbit-like babies the first time. Procreation became a side gig. Though I felt back on track, my wheels were spinning on oil. I didn't see how we could progress. What changed this month? Nothing. Already doing everything they advised. Why should I succeed? Negative test, negative test.

I struggled to accept each disappointment as my inability to conceive stretched into an unending future. Chris was with me, yet I felt alone again. One day, I randomly asked my social media followers whether they had miscarriage or infertility tales. Responses poured in.

I met scores of women and men and learned about miscarriage, IVF, polycystic ovarian syndrome, endometriosis, and adoption. I heard from couples who kept trying after a decade and those who gave up after years of failure.

This openness impacted me so much that I developed a miniseries about infertility on my podcast Labyrinths with Chris, where we relate stories about how we can become lost and find our way again. Without my consent, I was accepted into another hidden organization of women—those who have lost pregnancies. I shed what could have been a baby in a private ceremony. For the thousandth time, as I had when I first attended the Innocence Network Conference, I recognized that being alone in misery was a choice I'd made, one society had promoted. I could also share my sadness with strangers to help them overcome trauma as they did mine. We often don't open ourselves because we think we can't fix someone else's private anguish, but expressing ourselves shows that you're not alone.

That didn't mean I was ready to tell Giuliano this. Being vulnerable with strangers and podcast listeners was one thing. Giuliano made me feel vulnerable just talking about my kitties.

After my first miscarriage, I got pregnant again, but I rejoiced more tentatively—it wasn't genuine until I heard a baby scream. I don't know if every pregnant woman does this, but at the end of my second trimester, I realized the kid in my womb wouldn't fit through any of my body's openings as I knew them. How have women given birth through their vaginas since the beginning of time? For real. That was impossible. It was impossible. Being sliced in two like a horrible egg was all I could envisage. How could I live?

My final months of pregnancy were spent believing I would die in childbirth. I believed I wouldn't die thanks to modern medicine, but my body didn't. As I got bloated and the baby kept growing unnervingly, I alternated between excitement and fear. Like waiting for a verdict.

I was worried about more than childbirth mortality. After our wedding crumbled and the tabloids ridiculed us, Chris and I were concerned about hiding our pregnancy. We couldn't handle the idea that my pregnant belly and our baby could be used to demonize me. I struggled more than ever with being caught in the shadow of my darkest experience. I didn't want my future kid to be imprisoned in that darkness, so we did everything we could to hide her existence and protect her until we worked out how to construct a life and raise her so she wouldn't feel that weight. We told ourselves that, but I wondered if I deserved the heart-exploding joy a kid would bring. Life prepared me for disappointment.

Through my conversations with Giuliano, I tried to break that conditioning by redefining my past. I told him my sister Deanna had a son. "I am happy for Deanna," he wrote. I have fond recollections of her. She was kind to me during the trial." He said his niece had a daughter named after his mother. He wrote, "When I found out, I was very emotional because it will be like filling the void left by my mother on April 23, 2012. Don Saulo officiated the funeral at Santo Spirito Church, where I was baptized years earlier." Giuliano would be touched to know I was pregnant, but I couldn't stand to think about how it would feel to write to him if I miscarried again. I don't believe till the baby cries. Giuliano and I were close, but not close.

My growing pregnancy made me hesitant to go out. My mom's neighbors gave me a hand-knit blanket while I was visiting. We uncomfortably thanked them and shrank, paranoid rather than grateful. Who told them?! Seeing me enter my mom's house, did they assume? They were unaware of the secret. How about telling people? I missed out on another minor part of modern motherhood—pregnancy beauty images and Facebook announcements. I nagged baffled family members not to publish photos of me on social media or tell even their closest friends the wonderful news. I was afraid the tabloids would harass me—paparazzi had already staked over my house during the pandemic—and use this wonderful time to tarnish me: You know who will never have children? Meredith.

I was happy last week despite everything. Chris and I took the boat to my mom's place in West Seattle the day after my birthday in a sundress. I finally had that pregnant lady glow on a beautiful day. I suddenly had soaked panties staring at Puget Sound. First, I thought I peed. I removed my underwear and smelled them in a restroom stall. Not urine. Then what? I experienced no gush, like my water had broken. My contractions were absent. Instead, I felt uneasy. Was everything okay? What could go horribly wrong now?

Lying on the couch at Mom's house, I contacted my OB-GYN, who advised me not to take a ferry home even though my water hadn't burst and I wasn't in labor. Instead, I should relax and expect labor within 24 hours.

I judged myself all day, humiliated and unsure. What labor should feel like was unknown. Everyone told me labor is like your first orgasm. My water never broke, but abdominal aches hit me like waves at 11 p.m. I gasped for breath after each contraction because they were so intense. Yes, I knew.

Unfortunately, Chris could only assist me count intervals. He made jokes on the way to the hospital to distract me. I instantly told him to shut up and get me to my destination. An amazing and skilled nurse helped me get comfortable to brace for the pain and let the baby come more smoothly at the hospital. My mother soon arrived to comfort me.

Six and a half hours after my contractions began, Eureka Muse was born after five pushes. As the doctor placed her on my chest, I said, "I'm sorry." She was screaming, and I felt the urge to comfort her and the existential crisis of not being able to take her agony. I was thrilled to see her. She was flawless.

Was she? Chris pointed to a raised, white patch of skin on Eureka's hand as I held her against my breast, cooing, as the doctor removed the placenta and sewed up my vaginal tearing. "What is that?" he questioned the nurse.

Just vernix. "It will disappear," she said.

"It doesn't look like it will wipe off." Chris insisted.

A flash of displeasure. Why did Chris already criticize our child? "It's nothing," I said.

"She's perfect," Mom said.

Chris declined and resumed stroking my hair. After we moved to a postpartum recovery room, he looked again and pointed out the elevated, discolored skin.

"It's probably a birthmark," I said.

The nurse looked and replied, with a hard-to-place wonder, "Huh, I've never seen a mark like that. It also trails up her arm."

An archipelago of little, raised, discolored skin patches ran up Eureka's arm, and when we examined her, we spotted more on her chest and leg. Chris mentioned it immediately when the doctor examined her. It embarrassed me. My hypochondriac hubby. But the doctor halted as she looked closer. She answered just, "I need to get back to you on that."

Her leaving broke my heart. I looked at my little girl, who was doing fine. She grabbed my breast effortlessly. She slept peacefully. Only when nurses poked and drew blood did she complain. "She's great." Astonished, I repeated loudly. I could not imagine her being ill.

After the doctor returned, she was calm but solemn. "The patches on Eureka's skin follow Blaschko lines," she said. That is, the normally undetectable pattern of fetal skin development in the pregnancy. "This implies a genetic mutation and related conditions." On a white board near the bed, she scribbled Incontinentia pigmenti, the likely condition.

"What is that?"

She said, "It's a genetic disorder that affects the skin, hair, teeth, nails and central nervous system."

"But we tested for genetic disorders."

Sorry, not this one. Exceptionally rare."

Why? Why couldn't I just enjoy snuggling my daughter? Why wasn't she perfect? I felt like I had survived a near-death experience. I needed peace and time with my daughter. Instead, I listened to the doctor describe incontinentia pigmenti's symptoms, which included cerebral atrophy, severe intellectual incapacity, lifelong seizures, detached retinas, blindness, scoliosis, and nightmare teeth. Eureka may have brain damage. Heart, kidney concerns. Additionally, elevated, discolored skin patches would solidify into painful wart-like blisters. The doctor said, "We need to schedule an MRI and EEG immediately before you can leave the hospital."

The next two days were hazy. Several specialists sat across from us and addressed our countless questions in the postpartum room. Between visits, Chris studied incontinentia pigmenti extensively. Rare, one in a million. De novo mutations arise randomly, not from parents to children. This was unsettling because even if I hadn't passed on the mutation, I felt guilty for passing on my bad luck. The most prevalent symptom was skin lesions, although one in three to one in six children had brain, eye, and other organ abnormalities. Doe she have her brain altogether? Chance it. Will she have seizures? Chance it. I held Eureka, filled with love and fear. This was not my ideal parenthood. We always understood there was risk in having a child, but we were vigilant. We took every test and asked every question.

Now what? Our future unfolded before me. Daughter would be a veggie. Must one of us be a full-time nurse for our child? How could we afford that? Would the state help? We would spend our lives meeting her basic needs. Then what? What would happen to her without us? Would her life be worth living?

Chris emotionally withdrew when we voiced these concerns. I understood his thoughts. I thought so too. Had our baby damaged everything? Would it have been better had she not been born? And that humiliating, immature, repeating thought: Didn't I deserve a healthy baby? Hadn't I endured enough?

Still, holding her and looking at her, I felt loyalty and affection. Nothing was more essential than her. Like my mother, I would always support her. So would my family. I'd been through enough crises to know that I had to resist my urge to isolate and that my loved ones would help me cope. Chris kept our families updated via SMS. That was enough because we couldn't tackle this problem alone and it may not have a solution.

Doctors tested Eureka for two days. They pulled her from me and placed her in the MRI's chilly metal womb. Her head was wired with dozens of wires to scan her brainwaves. She rarely complained. If nothing else, we knew her brain was intact before leaving the hospital. That concludes it.

We went home in uncertainty. My first several months were like to prison. It was unclear what was wrong and how it would affect us. I sobbed breastfeeding her. Chris worried every sleep twitch was a seizure as he cradled her. We called every specialist—neurologist, ophthalmology, cardiology, dermatology, geneticist—hoping for the best but anticipating the worst. The brain matter was intact, her retinas were attached, her heart, kidneys, and bones were normal, and her lesions had partially receded.

Chris and I debated how and when to announce our daughter's arrival. We couldn't hide her forever. We knew my first child's birth would be a tabloid story. I accepted. Instead of letting the tabloids frame this personal growth in reference to the long narrative preceding it, we opted to tell our own tale on our podcast.

As we completed those podcast episodes, I thought about Giuliano. I understood that despite I had accepted this man into my life, which largely affected me and Chris, I would soon have to decide whether to let him into my child's life, and I could feel the decision coming.

Jessica Bennett of the New York Times wanted to write a major profile on how I stayed in a story after my acquittal. I'm delighted I could show the public how long false convictions last and how life doesn't return to normal after prison. That feature would debut in the fall alongside our pregnant podcast. The world would learn I had a daughter. I couldn't explain why, but I knew I should tell Giuliano first. Perhaps I was interested about his reaction. I sent him a photo of myself in the postpartum room with Eureka bundled and nuzzled into my arm three weeks after her birth, months before the podcast or New York Times profile. I requested his confidentiality and informed him she was a secret. I hadn't handed the Times that photo.

Giuliano rejoiced. "Finally, I see you happy without that shadow that you carry around," he wrote, "and I know I have contributed to your happiness. What beauty! Allowing someone into your private life shows affection, he stated. "I enjoy hiding this little girl's face. Keep it to myself. This is your best 'medicine.'"

It was good that he saw my excitement, but frustrating that he couldn't see that his actions had left me scarred and that no amount of joy could remove that. Naturally, he didn't know about Eureka's diagnosis's new shade over me.

Months later, the geneticist reported Eureka had no incontinentia pigmenti. The bad news: they didn't know Eureka's genetic mutation or potential symptoms. It was no small matter. As Blaschko-like, it was solely similar to incontinentia pigmenti and epidermal nevus. It could be a birthmark-like skin lesion for life or something worse.

I have to embrace uncertainty as a fundamental premise of my existence in prison. I had to endure that again, but for my daughter and family. I was unnervingly grateful for my Perugia experience again. I utilized this to help Chris, my mom, and my family cope with uncertainty.

Chris and I came up with unique strategies to help Eureka view her pathology positively. Part dragon, she is! Dragon scales covered her arm. She might have magical powers one day. My eternal hunt for silver linings saw this issue as a possible solution for Eureka, who was incredibly lovely except for this small patch of rough and discolored skin on her palm. She possessed a beauty that would be detrimental for her self-esteem, therefore I thought those dragon scales would remind her not to love her appearance too much. If those skin lesions were her only ailment, Chris and I felt ready to help her build her self-image. More serious issues would be addressed as a family. We'd support her no matter what. Like my family was for me.

CHAPTER 29
Life Isn't Fair

During my first months caring for my possibly terribly damaged but increasingly healthy and typical newborn, my correspondence with Giuliano reduced, but he reached out on October 4, my release anniversary. He wrote, "For me, at the time, it was a defeat, but today I'm happy for you. I kiss the baby and embrace you."

"Every year, this is a day of reflection for me," I replied. "I appreciate being free and alive. As a mother, I feel Meredith's and my mother's grief.

I screamed in my head a few weeks inside prison after my mom gave me such a happy, pain-free childhood: Why? Why am I experiencing this? Is my balance due? Was tragedy making up for years of neglect by inflicting twenty years of suffering in weeks? This thought predated my conviction and 26-year sentence.

I wanted my daughter to realize that life wasn't fair and that no one deserved my suffering or Meredith's and her family's destiny. No one deserves cancer or an earthquake-killed child. Traumas are inevitable, but we don't deserve a pain-free life. Nothing's certain. Because we don't deserve our tragedies or joys, we can see compassion as a right. We all struggle with life's randomness. We don't pick our genes, circumstances, talents, or shortcomings. Allow each other some leeway. My parents taught me that, which helped me endure prison and recognize the humanity in my fellow convicts and prosecutor.

I wondered how Eureka would learn about my background as we exchanged letters with Giuliano. Despite my best efforts, I worried that she would live in the shadow of my erroneous conviction and that the media content mill that objectified me would objectify her. Despite my trauma-shaped concern for her, I wanted her to feel free. Pain will happen to everyone, but I hoped she wouldn't have to struggle for it and that freedom would be as natural as air. As my mother wished, I wanted her to be nice to herself and others, especially in difficult times. I wanted her to be a woman who helped her attackers.

With the pandemic ending, I wanted to meet Giuliano in person. I proposed June and invited Eureka to meet her.

He agreed, and I kept sending him photos and telling him about my baby, who was learning to eat kiwi and peanut butter, reading to her in Italian and German, and teaching her sign language. Giuliano proposed a public event hosted by a trusted journalist in spring 2022 as we discussed logistics. I knew this meeting would be unique. I knew it would be unusual and tense, but valuable for me and anyone who felt like they were confronting an intractable enemy or pain from the past. If I could cross that dangerous bridge, others might too. Most of us don't have prosecutors, but we do have alienated family, exes, and unhealed scars that throb when we hear a song or pass a restaurant. Giuliano wanted our encounter to impact more than just us. Though I wanted that, I understood the media couldn't be engaged. Meeting in public or with a journalist would influence our conversation. Giuliano might be less honest with me in front of an audience. I scared I would freeze up in front of a stranger. I suggested a private meeting with just myself, Giuliano, and Don Saulo, who knew us and could mediate.

After booking my trip, I had to take a breather from the laptop. A long-held hypothesis has become real. I was returning to Perugia to see my jailer. I brought my daughter. Conflicting feelings flooded me. I felt excited, afraid, proud, and possibly crazy. What was wrong with me? Just why did I care about Giuliano Mignini thoughts? Did I have Stockholm syndrome? Why couldn't I let him be wrong across the world? He couldn't hurt me further unless I did what I was evidently doing, putting my heart in his grasp.

It didn't help that my family believed it was a horrible, possibly hazardous notion. I received a video from my stepdad showing Giuliano and other panelists, who were plainly engaged in my guilt, criticizing my 2015 acquittal's rationale and legality. He stated they overstepped their boundaries talking about evidence and encroached on merits courts' authority. "It rather departs from lawfulness." He publicly argued that the Court of Cassation verdict that acquitted Raffaele and myself was a miscarriage of justice and a violation of legal precedent that should never have happened.

My panic began. Could he have lied to me all along? Prosecutor or nice uncle,h Giuliano? My stepdad thought Giuliano was trying to get me jailed again in Italy. I couldn't rule out that possibility. My family hadn't met him like I had. They kept telling themselves he was nasty, corrupt, an idiot, and a coward. They hadn't seen him and weren't interested in hearing what I'd learnt from listening. Truly listening to someone is powerful, both healing and harmful. Those who know us best can hurt us most. However, they know where and how to treat our wounds. I understood this intuitively as a young adult, but I learnt it in prison. People will tell you who they are if you just listen and stop telling yourself who you want them to be.

There was no going back. Exactly why I was doing this was unclear. I felt it was crucial. Though scary and challenging, knowing how hard it was drove me. I might be a masochist. I kept questioning myself as the meeting approached. I hoped for what? An apology, recognition of wrong, and promise to defend my innocence? It all felt silly and superficial. Why put myself psychologically, emotionally, and legally at risk? What would I gain by risking?

I asked myself the wrong questions.

CHAPTER 30
Preemptive Closure

I like to solve problems, check boxes, and finalize plans. So as I counted the days until my meeting with Giuliano, I worked on my travel itinerary, packing list, and emergency escape plans if the paparazzi found me in Italy. Answering those questions was easier than answering the Big Question: Why sit down face-to-face with my opponent, who had become what during the pandemic? Friend? A friend? An ally? It was hard to characterize Giuliano and my connection. Perhaps not pushing that connection to be anything helped it blossom. I had no idea if it would disintegrate when I entered a room with him because it had grown at a safe six thousand kilometers away. The nervousness of staring at a blank page in a notepad before writing a poem or an empty canvas with a paintbrush was familiar. I'm not a great poet or painter, but I've tried enough to understand that art is impossible without a strategy or vision. You must faith that the effort will yield something.

I took all these worries to a speaking engagement where I was to share my story with a group of entrepreneurs and business leaders. I accepted a while ago and regretted it less than a month before my Perugia trip.

Like my Modena speech, I ended my talk by saying I had learnt to see Giuliano's humanity and wished to understand him beyond what he had done to me. I informed the room that I had ordered tickets and would sit across from him, requesting anonymity. I cried and said:

I don't know what's going to happen. I don't know what to expect. But the difference between me now and me then is that I can do something. Back then I was helpless. Now I have agency, and I can choose to do something that feels right. I'm trying to figure out the answer to a lot of really hard questions, in part for Eureka, because it's one thing for me to live in the shadow of the worst thing that I never did. It's another thing for her to. I know that up to this point, I haven't really accomplished much. But I have done what my mother asked me as a kid. All I can do is be kind. Because I can. I can be kind. No one can stop me! And so that's what I'm going to do, and that's the model I'm going to hold and share with my daughter.

I was recommended by my host to ask this group of accomplished businesspeople for advice. I didn't know what to ask, but I'd listen to advice.

A silver-haired man with warm eyes asked the first question after the clapping. He was honored to help me and stated he was great at it.

Chris, Eureka, and I headed home fatigued the next morning from the dramatic experience. I was ready to start logistical preparation again, answering easy questions instead of challenging ones, when the silver-haired man, David Zelman, emailed me to visit me before my trip to Perugia. I was astonished, but we scheduled it. He seemed like a business counselor, so I figured he wanted to help Chris and me make money writing and podcasting. David didn't want to give me career advise.

Before we returned to my house from the airport, he said, "I'm offering you closure with your prosecutor, your trauma, and all that happened to you in Italy by the conclusion of this weekend. You can accomplish that without meeting him in Perugia. You can do now."

It was a bold claim, and I was doubtful. Chris and I visited David last weekend. We hiked and prepared dinner, but we basically sat and talked for hours. After a life change, David became a psychotherapist and wrote If I Can, You Can. He now coaches corporate leaders in personal growth and well-being. I didn't know much about that environment or Werner Erhard and Byron Katie, who affected David's work.

Author and lecturer Erhard popularized self-improvement and training seminars in the early 1970s. His realization was epiphanic. He told his biographer, "It was so stupidly, blindingly simple that I couldn't believe it. I realized there were no hidden meanings, everything was as it should be, and I was fine. I recognized I was not my thoughts or emotions. I was not my thoughts, intelligence, perceptions, or beliefs." Byron Katie, a late-80s self-improvement teacher, had an insight that helped her overcome depression and drug misuse. "I found that believing my thoughts hurt me, but not believing them didn't hurt me, and this is true for everyone. Freedom is simple. I learned suffering is optional."

David had his own insight and phrased his ideas differently. I didn't realize it then, but David was giving me Zen Buddhist wisdom. Indeed, Erhard was close friends with Alan Watts, the zany philosopher who popularized Zen Buddhism in the West in the 1960s. This was my developing fascination. Since the pandemic began, Chris and I had been using the Waking Up meditation app, which focused on noticing consciousness before thoughts and emotions, which arrive and leave on their own. It goes beyond breathing or "quieting the mind." To clearly notice how ideas and emotions develop without judgment and know that you are not your mind's buzzing swirl of anxieties, expectations, hopes, and fears is the goal.

David gave me two critical ideas that weekend. 1. Everyone has their own reality, and you must know how it differs from yours to act accordingly. If a child wants to touch a snake, remember that in their world, there is no danger. Danger is in your perception. Recognizing that makes you stop the youngster from being bitten. As I prepared to meet Giuliano, I had to confront his reality. We wouldn't succeed if I pretended we shared the same world and truths. Accepting that he thought he did nothing wrong.

Accepting meant acknowledging, not condemning. I have to let his personal reality guide my interactions with him. Although I knew Giuliano had made many mistakes, some of which were hurtful to me and others, I realized that trying to convince him otherwise would only cause confrontation and defensiveness.

David also taught me that I didn't need Giuliano's answers, apologies, or explanations. "If you go there hoping to get something from him, you are setting yourself up to fail," David cautioned. "Telling yourself you need something from him gives him power over you." I had been meditating for years and obsessing over these concerns, but it hit me then. He was right. Would I live with an open wound for the rest of my life if Giuliano never apologized or accepted fault? All because one man couldn't admit he was wrong? That only affected my health if I let it. Simple as that.

This Zen-like approach favors activity and simplicity. Avoid overcomplication. Hearing it when you're used to overthinking everything is unpleasant.

"But how do I stop caring?"

What made you care? David asks. You just do."

I remembered Yoda: "Do or do not. No attempt." It wasn't about learning how, but doing it. I had made that mistake a million times: mistaking willpower failure for doubt about how to achieve anything. You can ponder, brainstorm, and debate which steps will solve your own difficulties, or you can repair them. You can opt to release.

This understanding came to me abruptly, like my prison epiphany, but it required weeks to comprehend, think out its consequences, and let it affect my behavior. It left me wondering: If I didn't need Giuliano to say or do anything to feel at ease, then was I stressing out to travel back to Italy to see him? Why bother if I had nothing to gain?

"Maybe you have something to give," David said. He gave me a controversial task in the end. "This might be challenging to hear," he added, "but I want you to ask yourself if there are any ways that you are grateful for how Giuliano Mignini shaped your life."

Part of me wanted to shout, "Fuck right off!" immediately. I anticipated parental disapproval: "I can't believe you're willing to talk to that monster."

"Fuck that asshole."

"He lied to you. It traps."

"He's using you."

"He belongs in prison."

But I remembered what Mom had taught me about kindness and what I knew was part of my mission in building this friendship. I returned to Perugia to be kind and make him feel seen. I had it in me, not because he deserved it. As a victim of a foreign justice system and vicious media, I felt powerless my whole adult life. Everyone associated my name with a horrific crime I didn't commit or a tragedy I suffered. None of these defined me. However, this was no survival or reaction to someone else's behavior. There was no need for this gathering. I caused it. Radical empathy and compassion reflected who I am. I felt empowered for the first time in this horrific story. I would offer Giuliano something in Perugia, get nothing from him. What exactly? I was unsure.

CHAPTER 31
Homecoming

Traveling to Modena taught me. Chris and I flew into Zurich and rented a car to cross the border to dodge the media. We moved through unimpeded. Again, my mom traveled with us to Italy to help with Eureka and introduce me to her friends from my time in a cell. Also, her lifelong policy of never allowing me visit Italy without her again. Florence was our lunch stop on the way south so Eureka could stroll. I always wore big sunglasses and a sun hat outside the car. If I were famous, paparazzi would swarm us. If that happened, we would cancel the meeting, drive back to Switzerland. Pushing my baby through Florence with Chris and Mom, I was nervous.

Being around Italian language and culture triggered me. However, summer brought a stream of tourists walking along the Arno to photograph the Duomo. Chris called me Marie when he needed to draw my attention in public, and I felt like just another American tourist. Still, I wouldn't remove those sunglasses.

I was also preoccupied, thinking ahead to my conversation with Giuliano or backward, remembering every time I sought to talk to him during my interrogation, inquiry, and trial and was ignored. For the trip, Chris and I said, Make good memories. I linked this country to trauma and injustice, but I also had fond memories of visiting Italy with my family as a teenager, touring Pompeii and excitedly telling Mom Latin textbook facts, and making dinner with my roommates in Perugia. Without declaring it as a mission, I realized I wanted to recapture Italy. That included seeing locations and meeting people who influenced my mom.

We drove 30 minutes from Perugia to Piegaro, a mountain village, via a meandering route that evening. Mom set up a safe house. We planned to stay there for a few days while I prepared for the meeting. Chris was more privacy-conscious than me. He continued asking Mom, "You sure you can trust these people?"

My heart fell for Piegaro immediately. The small, cobbled alleys, constructed for walkers and carts, barely big enough for modern cars; the unexpected alcoves and stairwells where village cats rested in the sun; the town's only bakery, butcher store, and café. It was a medieval community built without a plan, with little stone homes and streets that followed the hillside. The Umbrian countryside, Italy's green heart, with breathtaking vistas of neighboring tiny towns' valleys and hills from almost everywhere.

Colleen, Mom's friend, led us through the winding alleys to our sanctuary, a small flat she and Tom restored from an 800s glass factory. Colleen and Tom, from Seattle, retired from law and design and bought an abandoned building to turn into a vacation rental in this tiny hamlet of 300 people.

Colleen offered us the flat for free, and I discovered she had done so before. I had six hours of visiting a month in prison, and my family made sure to attend every visit for four years. That was tough and expensive to organize. Thank goodness my stepdad, a computer security expert, could operate remotely. Mom visited only during elementary school breaks. My stepdad lived in Italy for months alone to make those hour-long trips. My family initially booked accommodations in an agriturismo an hour from the prison.

Colleen told me about her connection to my family over wine that night. One day, an Italian acquaintance who owned a local winery asked her, "What do you know about that young woman over in Capanne prison?" Colleen: Amanda Knox? Her innocence is clear. This is crazy." Her friend agreed and that Colleen contact Sabina Castelfranco, a journalist who had been familiar with my family.

Sabina told my stepdad, "I have a place 20 minutes from Capanne." Free housing is available here. Just come."

My stepdad came that evening and lived in Colleen and Tom's Piegaro flat for my last year in prison. Mom remained there when she could get off work. A stranger helped because she could. The result was inspiring. However, I apologized to Colleen for being cold and robotic. Crisis makes me withdraw. I call it "going dead possum." Despite myself, I sensed the Giuliano meeting approaching.

These people helped my family and became friends. Just as she wanted to relax on the balcony overlooking the hills and toast the setting sun with an Aperol spritz, Mom wanted to share that with me. We made her emotional. She claimed, "I would sit here, day after day, staring out at this beautiful view, drinking wine and feeling guilty as hell," knowing her baby was 20 minutes away in a cage.

"To making good memories," I murmured, raising my glass. Mom and Chris were beside me as swallows flew through the dusk light and Eureka played with a flower. A moment of heaven. I fantasized about moving here with my family and opening a shop. We'd eat ripe tomatoes and drink wine in peace and meditation. Naturally, that cement and barbed wire complex over the next hill called to me.

After my Friday appointment with Giuliano, Mom, Chris, and Eureka took me to Capanne on Thursday morning. Not sure why I had to view it. I went in a hurry, never expecting to return. Perhaps I wanted to experience Mom approaching that fence. On the winding roads between Piegaro and the prison, which also went to Perugia and cut through olive groves, vineyards, old stone walls, and towers peeking above umbrella pines and cypress trees, I thought I had driven these roads a hundred times to the courthouse but never seen them because I was in the windowless prison van.

After the roundabout, we stopped in the parking lot. I exited to assess the situation. My mind filled with inner sights immediately. The long, echoing hallway, mad institution doors, barred windows, and cement-walled yard where I circled endlessly. It did not appear to be a prison. Gray structures, a gated entry, barbed-wire fence. A military base, government research center, or business defense contractor could have been it. But inside that barbed-wire fence, behind those cement walls, individuals I knew were still rotting away, having not departed since I was hustled out of my cell eleven years earlier.

After about five minutes, I felt enraged. I kept shaking my head as we drove away, amazed that I had spent four years there. The fact that I had to wonder how to live a meaningful life in that cement box for 26 years made me angry. I was enraged at the emotional and mental acrobatics I had to do to survive that horrible wound in the Italian countryside.

The years inside were like living in a time-and-spaceless realm. But seeing it lying there, drab and plain, at some random turnoff in the middle of nowhere, made it seem mundane. Just a place that stole years of my life. How trivial and meaningless. witnessing Capanne from outside was unlike witnessing a cathedral. No amazement, blah.

As I prepared to meet Giuliano, I wasn't sure if this visit was helpful. It called to me, and I wasn't in Italy to ignore it. The loudest call came from Perugia. I knew it was time to return to the city I'd called home for five weeks.

I was frightened in the Piegaro café that morning. Chris and I had coffee at six a.m., me in my sunglasses and cap. Eureka crawled on the front cobblestones while Mom dressed. A quiet morning in a sleepy town meant only a few people were up, so I took off my sunglasses as I picked up my cappuccino because it was hard to see inside. An older woman in the café looked at me and asked, "Are you Amanda?"

I felt like a pantry mouse that couldn't leave fast enough. "I'm Marie," I murmured hesitantly, "from California," and went outside to a patio table, retreating into my sun hat and glasses.

Colleen told us of a local older woman with a small dog who was a friend. She didn't know I was coming. She had no idea she would see Amanda Knox in Piegaro that day, but like millions of people, especially in Italy, she knew my face like her own. Because I felt sorry for lying to her, I wanted Colleen to apologize and ask her to keep my presence in Italy a secret.

After arriving in Perugia, I didn't want to leave the automobile. Mom wanted a spritz at the Brufani hotel, and I remembered how one of my lawyers, Carlo, had always dreamed of my returning to Italy and parading along Perugia with my head held high. Even if part of me wanted to say, "I can be here as much as anyone!" I'm not ashamed or terrified! I realized the consequences of being caught. It would be front-page news, and the journalists would follow me back into Switzerland.

Our driving tour of the city was as stunning as I remembered. The medieval city is a maze of steep and twisting alleyways that lead to Etruscan-era piazzas, aqueducts, and archways on a hill and overflowing into the valley below. Ivy-covered buildings are decorated like pastel Easter eggs. Tall and narrow passageways hide the sky unless you look high. Popes, painters, peasants, and students tore into the stone stairways over centuries. So many pupils. The University of Perugia, founded in 1308, and the University for Foreigners, where I studied, are in town.

I felt déjà vu walking past the old travertine wall. I had never driven these streets, only walked them, so time had added unfamiliarity to the surprisingly familiar. The city I recalled appeared unexpectedly. The university and my bookshop appeared as we turned a corner. "See where I got coffee!" We were soon driving down the small hairpin turn adjacent to the basketball courts, the strip without a sidewalk where I had to evade fast mopeds on my way home from class. There it was: Via della Pergola 7.

There was construction ahead, so we passed slowly. We saw the terrace where Meredith and I read and played guitar in the afternoons, overlooking the valley and eating stone fruits and chocolate. Someone hung washing there. Naturally, someone else lived there now.

Strangely, someone presumably napped in Meredith's murder room. They showered in Rudy Guede's gory bathroom.

The city was full of tourists and students, but as we drove back to Piegaro, I felt calm. I felt sad and pity for my twenty-year-old self. I was having the time of my life in Perugia. I was a kid and was captivated by this metropolis that invited me to explore and grow. I felt gorgeous, and then I met Raffaele, making everything perfect. Until not. I tried to recall those early, joyful days, but I couldn't without thinking about what followed next. Peace accompanied this silence. Seeing that laundry waving in the gentle air, I understood Perugia and Via della Pergola 7 were merely places. It was where a terrible incident happened, but also where young couples fell in love, babies were born, and poems were written.

I was happy in Perugia before it got sad and horrible. It was someone else's optimism or excitement even then. Everyone had a good and horrible place. Every beautiful winding road brought the mother of a careless motorist grief. Every peaceful park saw marriage proposals and heartbreaking breakups. Perugia and the house surpassed their events. I didn't have to feel anguish or grief there unless I held onto it. It might be therapeutic and beautiful if I wanted it to be. The choice was mine.

CHAPTER 32
Faccia a Faccia

Mom had been spilling her worries about the meeting with Giuliano throughout the trip, adding subtle notes at the end of discussions. The night before, it all came to a head. "I don't trust this human being at all," she remarked.

She and my stepdad believed Giuliano was lying to me and that the two years of contact, which she had not seen, were a ruse to get me back to Italy. He might try to arrest me on additional charges in the worst instance. Ideally, he would exploit me and use our meeting. My mom experienced a life-shattering experience when this man wrongfully imprisoned her daughter. She also witnessed the Italian justice system's petty, vengeful, and absurdity. She still remembered being arrested on Giuliano's orders, brought to an office, handcuffed, and charged with slander against the police for repeating to the press what I had told her about being slapped in the back of the head during my interrogation. After all that, she wasn't crazy to care about further baseless accusations.

Like my mom, I worried Giuliano was lying to me. Before our departure, retired FBI Special Agent Steve Moore, who helped me escape Italy in 2011, warned us he had found something disturbing. In his study, he found that five days before Meredith was slain, Perugia police had alerted Milan police about Rudy Guede burglarizing a nursery school in Milan, and Guede was freed without charges. Why in the world did it happen? Steve believed Rudy Guede was a Perugia police criminal informant, possibly for Giuliano Mignini, but couldn't prove it. Releasing Guede from that little crime was disastrous since he murdered Meredith days later. If so, Perugia officials would have put Meredith's murder on someone else, and since they already had Raffaele and myself in arrest when they determined Guede was the culprit, we would be blamed. According to Steve, Giuliano Mignini had to lie about a sex game gone bad to imprison two innocent people and give Guede a lighter charge to cover for himself or his colleagues. Steve's theory was terrifying despite its uncertainty.

Eureka undoubtedly wondered what was up with the room's tension and why I wasn't reading with her.

Mom remarked, "I always imagined him hearing a little voice in his head, saying, 'This is bullshit. You're wrong.' He ignored that voice."

"But ignoring that voice doesn't mean he's evil," I said. "It could mean he lacks moral courage to act right."

"So he's a coward!" Mom exclaimed. She was still upset with Giuliano, and even though I had convinced her not to call him evil, she was determined to label him otherwise.

"It also tells you something about the nature of the world," Chris said. "Learning that someone who's not evil can cause life-crushing harm changes your view of harm. And how to reduce and prevent harm."

One of many reasons I adored Chris. We had an unusual worldview: giving everyone the benefit of the doubt and realizing that compassion equals strength.

When we went to bed, I was still doubtful. "No one thinks I'm doing the right thing here," I added. "My mom, family, Steve, and lawyers don't. My stepdad calls him 'Pignini.' Not helpful." Why that made people feel better eluded me. So universal. Name calling doesn't heal, and it didn't make me feel better.

Dehumanizing insults are intended. My stepdad meant that Giuliano wasn't human, hadn't behaved like a human, and couldn't develop or change. Ironically, Giuliano's treatment of me was human. Humans make mistakes often. Cowardly and egotistical, we self-delude and protect our egos at all costs, even if it hurts innocent people. Fucking each other. Pigs don't.

Despite my reservations, I was confident Giuliano's cunning or cowardice didn't matter. The judgment was about him. He escaped my grip. Only I could control myself. I felt like I was testing myself to see who I was. Without risking pain, I couldn't receive the prize of my courage in this situation.

I meditated at the window before dawn as birds flew over the valley chasing insects in thermals. Sunlight from somewhere unseen touched the green hills to the west. As calm and determined as I had felt in a long time, I felt anxiety-free. I was going to do something scary, but I was not turning back.

Don Saulo had arranged a meeting at Villa Sacro Cuore, a church-owned hotel outside Perugia, for Giuliano and me. After twenty minutes of winding through the hills, we reached the villa's unpaved and rocky road, which slowly gave way to a manicured lawn, tall umbrella pines, and a large, elegant building painted yellow—my favorite color—on a hill overlooking the valley south of Perugia. Since we arrived 30 minutes early, I assumed Giuliano and Don Saulo hadn't arrived. Mom refused to go in, so we gave her the rental car for a drive.

It was unclear how long this meeting would go. But she took her book and found a bench on the grass a few dozen yards from the building. Chris and I entered the lobby with Eureka.

I approached the desk and reluctantly informed the woman that I was seeking Don Saulo. She said, "Sì, certo, ti stavamo aspettando. Still no Saulo. Want a coffee? Of course, we expected you. Saulo hasn't arrived. Would you like coffee? She took us upstairs to a small conference room and made us two cappuccinos.

This was the first Peruvian resident who knew who I was. She was so lovely and loving that I cried. Perugians took images of themselves waving "Perugia vi odia" signs online after my acquittal. Perugia hates you. Not expecting this woman or anyone in Perugia to be kind. I anticipated the reverse. I always anticipated the opposite.

Some walls of the meeting room had literature, while others had portraits of recent popes: Jean Paul II, Benedict, Francis. Chris could hang out with Eureka in a bedroom next to the meeting room while I sat with Giuliano.

This chamber would host it. His and my relationship would dissolve in seconds. I had last spoken to him in the makeshift courtroom at Capanne a few days into my imprisonment, where I desperately tried to explain that this was all a big misunderstanding. He had pounced on my every word, trying to entrap me in some incriminating admission.

I checked my notes and realized I needed to look up a word. I forgot how to say "grief" in Italian. The reason was evident when I checked it up. Grief has no name. Italians say "dolore." Pain. Naturally, grief is anguish for something lost. To say, "I grieve for somebody," use "piangere," which means "to cry." I instantly realized how much the language structure had set me up to be misinterpreted. Italians are known for their expressiveness in joy, excitement, and grief. I was seen as cold, unmoved, weird, and suspicious following Meredith's death since I was numb and not crying much. I wanted to bridge my relationship with Giuliano, which went beyond prosecutor and defendant. As profound as language.

Chris looked out the side window when a car pulled up. We saw Don Saulo and Giuliano on the terrace talking. We couldn't hear them, but Don Saulo appeared to be instructing Giuliano. Before entering, they waited five minutes outside.

Mom sat on the bench under a tree, but she didn't read. She hyperventilated. I didn't know this, but she told me she panicked for hours thereafter. A siren blared in the distance, and she knew Giuliano Mignini had set his trap, made the call, and was going to arrest me for some manufactured accusation to steal her daughter again.

As the footsteps echoed up the stairway, I was scared of something else: that my confidence would fail me, that anger, despair, or tears would overcome me, that I wouldn't be able to talk to Giuliano with love. I pulled myself together, and Don Saulo entered with Giuliano behind him. I collapsed.

Don Saulo was warm, his eyes sparkled, and he looked as if he hadn't aged since I last saw him playing music in his office while I awaited my release. I had spent so much time intellectually and emotionally preparing for Giuliano that I hadn't considered seeing Don Saulo again. I hugged him and cried on his shoulder for a minute. He was my closest buddy in my worst hour, a source of amazing kindness and generosity in a horrible place. He was still strong after years of serving the traumatized in prison.

Giuliano patiently waited behind us until we release our grip. So much for not crying. Finally, I turned to him and saw that he was as tall as I remembered, but less imposing, with a scraggly ring of gray hair around his bald forehead and a wounded animal smile. His casual attire surprised me. Not only did I not anticipate him to wear the black robes he had worn in court, but also a cargo vest like he had just returned from fishing. "It's okay," he said in Italian. "Calm your butterflies."

I introduced him to Chris and Eureka, who mirrored Giuliano's kindness. She was unaware of this man and filled the gap between us. I wasn't sure how to greet him. We didn't hug or shake hands, but he offered Eureka his finger. A star-shaped music box with a draw string was his gift to her. It delighted her.

We chatted about my trip from the US and Villa Sacro Cuore's beauty, then Chris and Eureka went to the adjoining bedroom while Don Saulo, Giuliano, and I sat at one end of the long table.

I was going to start by saying, "I'm here to listen to whatever it is that you have to say," but Don Saulo started it. Amanda wants to tell you something, so please listen without interrupting. I instantly had to start this conversation. Don Saulo, who was sitting next to Giuliano, rose and sat next to me across the table. I cried for 15 minutes as Don Saulo stroked my hair and petted me like a nervous bunny. Italian: I looked Giuliano in the eyes and said:

I want you to know I'm innocent. I had nothing to do with Meredith's murder. You were wrong about me. I was treated as if I were guilty until and unless I could convince you and your colleagues of my innocence. And I failed to do that. But I am not here to convince you of my innocence. I am here to let you know that whether you've realized your mistake or not, I do not think you are an evil person.

My breath escaped me, and I tried to regain control of myself. At that moment, Giuliano was tearing up as well. He reached out and took my hand and held it in both of his. My brain could not even process this, but I pushed through:

Your mistake, which caused great harm to me and my loved ones, and to Raffaele and his loved ones, is not the only thing that defines you. I want you to know that although I am still hurt today, I am grateful for my experience, in which you played an important and influential role. I am grateful because I learned things about myself that I never would have known: both how weak and vulnerable I am, but also how strong. I am a very strong person. I know this is largely because of you. This experience crystallized for me my core values: curiosity, compassion, and courage. Curiosity for the truth, not just the version that most serves me. Compassion, especially for those who have made mistakes. And courage to overcome my own fears and pain to remain curious and compassionate toward others, especially those who have harmed me. We cannot change the past, but we can change the future. And the mistakes of our past are the opportunities of our future. It is never too late to live our values. And I believe you are a person of value. I do not wish you ill. I wish you peace.

Giuliano squeezed my hand, eyes shining. "I'm also here to grieve," I said. I looked up this word last minute. "I went to Perugia as a naïve girl and returned home traumatized. After years, I've been able to understand what occurred and emerge from the ashes, but part of me died here, and I'm here to cry for her and maybe feel complete again."

As I told my prosecutor, the metaphor became physical. I felt like I was at the burial of my twenty-year-old self, the girl who had never been hurt. When I returned to Seattle, I believed I would shed my prison clothing like snakeskin and become that lively girl again. Of course I couldn't. She died. It took me this long to realize. I went to Perugia to see Giuliano, sprinkle her ashes, and say farewell.

Before Giuliano reacted, I felt victorious. After saying what I came to say, I felt like I was finally enacting a resilience truth: after major trauma, you can't go back to who you were, but you can shape who you become.

Giuliano replied, holding my hand. We talked 90 minutes and he never stopped. I cried a lot and had severe disagreements. In the chat, we jumped about, so I'll start with what he didn't say.

He didn't apologize. He didn't say "I was wrong." He never asked, "What can I do to make amends?" He did not say, "Please forgive me."

He said he followed the evidence and blamed his coworkers, especially the female cops. "Women can be vicious to other women," he remarked, "and female police officers hated you. I wasn't the one who first suspected you, but they targeted you, and by the time I arrived, I could only prosecute you."

He said the case always upset him because everyone held him accountable for his colleagues' behavior, even though the police were making decisions before he became involved and he wasn't the sole prosecutor. He claimed that he did not deny me a lawyer or keep me up all night throughout my interrogation. He was right. He stated he felt constrained by his responsibility and the evidence, which he said he investigated honestly. There were others like him doing the same job, which was unpleasant.

Asking Don Saulo to mediate this face-to-face meeting was probably my greatest move. He supported me throughout. He and Giuliano had known them other for decades, but Don Saulo knew how much occurred to me and wouldn't allow Giuliano sugarcoat anything. Giuliano recognized that the police mistreated me, but Don Saulo said, "What happened to Amanda in that interrogation was torture. They tortured her." Giuliano tried to connect with me by saying, "We both have been misrepresented as monsters. "We both suffered," Don Saulo said, "Yes, but Amanda spent four years in prison."

Giuliano said he couldn't have done anything differently. I tried to resist the idea that he was objective and logical while he made up a murder orgy scenario with no evidence. Don Saulo intervened when needed: "Giuliano, I need you to listen to Amanda now."

Despite my sensitive and sharp attempts to point out his flaws, Giuliano insisted that he had been logical and had followed the evidence. Don Saulo replied, "I've been telling you for years, Giuliano, that you have all your facts and evidence, but there must be another explanation, because Amanda is not capable of such harm."

"Well," Giuliano said, "one can make mistakes."

Giuliano had insisted on this in all his letters, so I wasn't shocked he repeated himself. He said, "That you would reach out to me after I asked for your condemnation is a truly heroic act," which surprised me. Only book characters do that." He stated he was thrilled to meet me and that I was his "favorite defendant." He said this sincerely while holding my hand. "Surreal" barely does it credit.

It went beyond praise. He said, "I was suffering when I asked that you be convicted." He said, "You are not the person I thought I was prosecuting."

"Do you think I'm innocent?" Asking him directly.

"I think you're telling me the truth."

"But can you admit my innocence?"

"If someone came to me today and asked me to prosecute this case, I would refuse. I know you cannot commit such a crime."

"So you admit my innocence."

„How many ways can I tell you what I think?" he asked.

I was stunned. Sbalordita. Giuliano seemed to think that even in retirement, he couldn't contradict his public deeds or dispute official rulings. "We must respect the Court of Cassation ruling," he repeated. His opinion was that the Italian legal system worked. The prosecution and defense balance each other at lesser courts before a verdict or sentence reaches the Court of Cassation. He was doing his job as the prosecutor, which is to prove guilt. To him, my four years in prison and eight years on trial were merely part of the legal system's truth-finding process. "The final ruling acquitted you, and I am happy you are free." He didn't seem to realize that he had a choice to prosecute me and that he decided to charge me with inadequate evidence and no rationale when the real killer was right in front of him.

However, my presence and this shared experience I produced for us moved him. He said "paradiso." Paradise. He considered this meeting one of his most precious experiences. He knew I had every reason to despise him, and he was moved that I didn't hate him and would go so far to connect with him. This feeling of his may have been exacerbated by my all-white attire and Eureka's presence. Did he suddenly see Madonna instead of a sneaky, bloodthirsty demon in court?

Despite his confidence in being analytical and objective, I suppose he obtained his original views by gut instinct, a terrible hunch. After years of trial, my lawyers and I tried to rationally argue against his claims. Now, I had reached him by passion and presence, not logic. The truth in my face changed his opinion of me, not because he had found a new logical reason. His dilemma was obvious. His "logical" beliefs clashed with his emotions, pride, and appropriateness. It was messy, and he was upset. But so was I.

My want to hear him accept culpability and my pity for his incapacity to do so conflicted every time the topic turned to the issue. Falling into a trap. I didn't want to condone his behavior, therefore shouldn't I expect accountability? Did I enable his belief that he did nothing wrong by saying, "I recognize your reasons for doing what you did"?

But not expecting anything from Giuliano was more than a stoic "admit what you can't control" attitude. It was about connecting through mercy and forgiveness without preconditions or true accountability and justice.

Instead of my harsh upbringing, I wanted a merciful world. From preschool to prison, punitive thinking permeates our lives. We confuse moral censure and castigation with the ability to establish an objective, authoritative, and intelligent opinion in the phrase "judgment." We're taught that right, wrong, blame, praise, reward, and punishment matter. When anything goes wrong, we are taught that the perpetrator is flawed and deserves punishment.

Prison confirmed an intuition. I'd long thought such sort of thinking was bad, but I felt righteous toward what I did and didn't deserve. I deserved no prison time! Never should I have been called a killer! But forcing Giuliano to confess culpability negated my goal. I was just defending him, which I knew was fearful. Of course he feared being wrong! Being mistaken about something so important in a society that joyfully punishes wrongdoers is unsettling.

After a long, confrontational, begging conversation where we talked past each other, I reverted to my original goal: to be kind to him.

"The justice system established us as enemies," I informed him. "Thank you for meeting me as a friend. I find that unusual, it reflects your character, and we may be an example. We can alter this tale. The story of the hideous girl who committed a horrible crime and the story of an innocent girl wrongly charged by a monster are currently believed. Both are false, but our story can continue. Write a new narrative together. As long as people doubt my innocence, they will speculate about me instead of honoring Meredith and holding Guede accountable, and the Kercher family will never find closure."

I wasn't sure if Giuliano would ever be able to do this, but I hoped that if I gave him a good image of himself and a chance to help affirm the truth and heal the Kerchers and everyone else hurt in this story, he would rise up and be his best.

He told me that people attacked me without knowing who I was, but now that he knew me, he would tell them. I'll tell people you're not a monster, and I hope you'll tell people I'm not.

"You made a terrible mistake," I repeated. I never wavered on this and will not let him forget it. I don't think that makes you bad. I wish you well." Then I hugged him.

He added, "I wish you well. To improve this for you."

We went outdoors into Villa Sacro Cuore's gardens with Chris and Eureka. Giuliano looked at my mom on the bench. He approached, but Mom saw him and ran for the car. He looked at me disappointed and confused. "Look," I said. My mother hasn't forgiven you. In her eyes, you placed her innocent daughter in prison for nothing she did."

Giuliano nodded knowingly. Had I forgiven him?

CHAPTER 33
A Dream Deferred

On November 2, 2007, I woke up in Raffaele's bed. The night before, we cooked, read Harry Potter in German, smoked a joint, made love, and watched Amélie, my favorite film. I had known this sweet, nerdy boy for a week, and we had fallen in love in a way that is only possible in the blissful unreality of a foreign fling, that fragile impermanent space where new love can blossom instantly, as if you'd found your soulmate, only because you both know, though you hide it from yourselves, that you will each return to your lives, alone and worlds apart.

We kissed and eagerly discussed our weekend plans in my bad Italian and his broken English. Raffaele planned to take me to truffle-loving Gubbio, a historic Umbrian town. We would spend a romantic weekend wandering the cobblestones, visiting cathedrals, and eating truffles! I never tried truffles. I imagined delicious mud. Due to having to shower and change clothes in my flat, I regretfully left. After 30 minutes, we'd be on our romantic getaway.

When I arrived home that morning, my apartment had been broken into, Meredith's door was locked, my two other roommates were gone, and something was seriously wrong. Five days later, I sobbed to sleep in prison. Reality crushed that Gubbio truffle dream like a childhood fairy tale.

We were tortured physically and psychologically during our interrogations. We were threatened with years in prison, denied bathroom breaks, sleep, and lawyers (Giuliano later claimed we were simply "witnesses," not "suspects," and not entitled to legal representation). The police believed I was hiding something, so they wore down Raffaele, my alibi for the murder, and forced him to sign a statement saying I left his flat and begged him to lie for me. He later relented.

My paramour became my co-defendant. Our trials led to decades in prison for him. Although the prosecution, media, and the world were captivated with Foxy Knoxy, he was Mr. Nobody. No one cared about him, a modest computer programming student with no history of violence who was uncomfortable and bashful around girls (which made me like him). Even his relatives knew he was a passenger. They advised him to put me under the bus after our conviction and appeal.

He might have made a deal with the prosecution, fled, and left me to die. That wasn't true. He valued truth as much as I did.

Raffaele owed me nothing, yet he was eager to face hell with me, even though I told him in our cell letters that our romance was gone and that I could no longer think of us that way.

It didn't bother him. For four years in prison, we only saw each other in court. Our friendship became linked, not romantic. Our destiny and life views were influenced by the same experience.

As hard as independence was for me, Raffaele had it worse. He remained in Italy. He was in his country while I faced extradition. He couldn't work, date, or avoid being the "boy accused of murder." Finally, the "boy re-convicted." I witnessed his Seattle reading of his memoir, which I also wrote. Sad reunion. The sword of Damocles still hung over us. We celebrated by phone after the Court of Cassation acquitted us. "Finished! The end! We're free!"

Since then, our lives have diverged. I had my partner Chris and my lovely daughter Eureka to lighten my days, while he was still looking for a career and family. We exchanged WhatsApp chats occasionally. I wouldn't say we were close, even if our relationship is permanent. Scar tissue is strong and sinewy.

When I returned to meet Giuliano, Raffaele was in Milan. I informed him of my plans, promised to report back, and suggested meeting up in Italy if I could stay undiscovered. After 15 years, driving past my apartment and along Raffaele's street in Perugia brought back vivid recollections. We lost a lot, including our naïveté, reputations, and even our old digital cameras that documented tender moments of passion. That trip to Gubbio seemed insignificant compared to all else we'd lost, a plan derailed by tragedy. However, Gubbio was only an hour from Perugia. No obstacle prevented us from ultimately traveling.

I called Raffaele and said, "Let's do it." We should eventually visit Gubbio and taste truffles." He drove five hours from Milan to meet me, Mom, Chris, and Eureka.

Raffaele pulled Eureka in the stroller while Chris and Mom walked behind us in the historic town, allowing us time to catch up and tell him about Giuliano. We planned a romantic Gubbio vacation 15 years ago, but this was different. I felt nostalgia for what could have been, thankfulness for my life, and regret for Raffaele, who was still seeking for many of my discoveries. Given the circumstances, he was kind to join me here and reinterpret this intimate encounter as familial.

Despite his eager gaze at me, Chris, and Eureka, he didn't hold it against me. I imagined a part of him thinking of that parallel universe where Meredith was never slain, we were never jailed, and we traveled to Gubbio that day. Perhaps many years later, happily married, we were going with our kid to revisit a location from our early romance. I certainly imagined that.

We entered a small piazza where a six-foot-tall clown was making faces at kids and tying balloon animals. Raffaele moved the stroller closer for Eureka. The clown exclaimed, "Che bella bambina," bending down. Is this your daughter? Beautiful tiny girl. Is this your daughter? "No," Raffaele said.

I wished I could help him. Give him love, family, children, and tranquility with my fingertips. But I knew he was on his own journey, like me, and our lives would continue to diverge. In Gubbio, coming together seemed like commemorating that love we felt fifteen years ago, the gauntlet we'd survived together, and who we'd become.

Naturally, we stopped at a café for truffles and got crostini with fresh tartufo, hummus, and cheese. Earthy, black, aromatic, and savory—wonderful dirt—the truffles were fantastic. Would my twenty-year-old self have liked them as much as I do now? I thought tartufo would be a good flavor for our tribulations, captivity, and struggle to find purpose. Nothing about that encounter was bright, acidic, or sweet. Initial taste was unpleasant and hard to swallow. But the woman I became through all that could taste how nutritious it was.

How's it? Chris questioned Raffaele while eating truffle crostini.

"Buono," he said. Good.

Raffaele had one more objective. Raffaele insisted we visit Assisi, a short trip from Gubbio. He wanted to see St. Francis' tomb. Catholic Raffaele wears a little cross around his neck. I knew his favorite saint was St. Francis of Assisi. 15 years earlier, he took me to Assisi in 2007, days before Meredith was murdered.

The tomb sits in a huge crypt underneath the Basilica of St. Francis, a white stone basilica with porticos that exudes clean, simple, and humble grandeur. Raffaele decided to make another visit. As we neared, he told us about St. Francis, the son of a wealthy silk trader who lived the rich kid life until a mysterious vision drove him to live in poverty, renovating medieval churches in the hills around Assisi. St. Francis patronized animals, the environment, and Italy. He protects against flames and dying alone. Raffaele may have prayed to him as we were chained to the stake.

Along with religious pilgrims, we went into the lower basilica, where ribbed vaults exhibited exquisite frescoes of St. Francis and other saints. Raffaele and I descended the narrow stairs to the burial chamber after leaving Eureka with Chris and Mom.

After paying our respects to the saint's bones, I returned to the stairs, but Raffaele wasn't ready. He promised to join me soon. He emerged after a few minutes and informed me what he was doing.

"The last time we were here," he added, "I prayed to St. Francis that we would always have happy memories together." Upon hearing that, my heart collapsed. A day or two before our arrest. "I think it was a curse," he laughed.

"What did you tell St. Francis this time?" I requested.

He said, "Forse non ci siamo capiti." Maybe we didn't comprehend.

I'm not Catholic, and I don't think anyone listens to such prayers, but I do think our lives are what we make them and that we can will ourselves into heaven or hell with enough conviction. A little puppy-loving Raffaele requested St. Francis for good memories for the two of us, but I don't think he believed it. But the Raffaele I saw that day chose light in darkness like I did. We would have nice recollections afterward. It was true if we wished it.

Chris, Mom, and I drove to Switzerland the next day. I got an email from Giuliano on the way.

Dear Amanda,

I have no words to describe what I felt at Villa Sacro Cuore. I hope it was a unique experience for you, too. Especially when we hugged. I will not forget it.

I was still processing the meeting with Giuliano, my reunion with Raffaele, and all the emotions I'd felt seeing Capanne prison and the house I shared with Meredith. I didn't have words either. As we crossed the border, I said aloud, "Ciao, Italia! Alla prossima!" Goodbye, Italy. See you next time! It was a casual phrase. The kind of thing one says absently when departing. But it felt true in the moment. There would be a next time.

CHAPTER 34
The Other Side of the Coin

While leaving Italy, I thought of Meredith and the quiet, daily moments we experienced in our weeks together. We trudged home from the grocery store, taking turns carrying heavy four-packs of two-liter water bottles uphill, dodging cars on tight street corners, sunbathing on the terrace, her reading a mystery novel while I played "Hey Ya" on the guitar, sipping espresso after class while Laura and Filomena, our Italian roommates, watched soap operas. I raced home to inform her about a hidden vintage store I found while walking. After we reunited, she bought a sparkling silver outfit for a New Year's celebration at home. I recall when she handed me her camera and requested me to take a picture of her by her bedroom window to show her family the valley below. She was effortlessly chic. I remembered loving her accent and how she felt like a big sister when she loaned me her tights. I remembered the last time I saw her, slinging her purse over her shoulder on her way to meet her British friends, waving farewell with a smile I'll never forget.

All these recollections feel close and distant today. Distance because I have to dig through nearly a decade of trauma to reach them. Before I can remember my fond memories of her, I must look past the autopsy photos and crime scene footage I saw, the slurs I was called, the death threats I received, the accusations I fought, the imprisonment I endured, and the slanderous headlines that unfairly linked our names and faces.

Meredith was a big part of my life when I first moved to Italy, so these memories are still dear. It may possibly be because I've never mourned her. I soon discovered in freedom that many assumed I couldn't mourn Meredith. They thought I was responsible for her murder or that Meredith was forgotten after my trials. Meredith and I were tightly tied, so my survival while she died was another injustice. To those noisy detractors, I could only vanish and quietly be grateful for life.

Meredith's family had a reasonable complaint when they continually turned to the media to revive interest in her and the justice she deserved. My name made news, not Meredith's. If I had been more clear early on, I would have said, "I agree!" If this case had been handled right, I would have been a footnote in this awful story like

Meredith's other two roommates, whom no one remembers. Meredith deserves justice and remembrance."

However, I couldn't believe that her murder and media erasure meant I should never talk about my suffering or that my battle for justice was a disrespect to her memory. It took me awhile to express this dilemma.

I call it single-victim fallacy. Crimes start with victims, like Meredith. By solving the crime and punishing the culprit, the authorities hope to comfort the victim's family. When they arrest and convict the wrong people, they create more victims. Raffaele, Patrick Lumumba, and moi. In their pursuit of the offender, the police held Patrick for two weeks based on an incoherent statement they compelled me into writing, despite his good alibi. They then closed his business for three months, which destroyed his life. The authorities pursued an unsubstantiated case against Raffaele and myself in their refusal to admit error. All three of us suffer more.

Because they compound victimhood and pit victims against each other, wrongful convictions distort our sympathies. The single victim fallacy holds that there is only one true victim in any event and that acknowledging the pain of an innocent prisoner is negating the victimhood of the slain. Not so.

This mistake is unfortunately common in wrongful conviction situations. The prosecution offers the initial victim's family a villain, and they accept it as part of their grief. When the conviction is overturned, they lose closure. This is why victims' families rarely support innocence claims.

I've contacted Meredith's relatives several times. I wrote them through their lawyer from prison. I sent them another letter after I arrived home and sent it through a journalist they knew. I've been reluctant to press farther because I know how difficult my existence must be to them, especially if they still think I killed Meredith. They may not realize it, but we've always supported them.

I rarely get asked how losing a buddy hurts. Meredith and I were young women in a new area at a comparable stage. We were studying, meeting people, and extending our worldview. We only knew each other for five weeks, but friendship, like romance, grows swiftly.

She and I often seem like two sides of the same coin. I got heads and she got tails on the coin flip. What happened to her might have happened to me. If I had been home that night, would she have found the crime scene, been wrongfully convicted, and be pondering all these years later, feeling lucky and sad?

If our roles were reversed, I would want her to survive, grow, and not let anyone take her life. She shouldn't be cowed by others who encourage her to disappear and be embarrassed of existing while her companion is dead.

I scarcely knew myself until I was arrested for murder. I was delicately figuring out who I was, who I wanted to be, and how I wanted to see myself. Later, the Italian courts and global media labeled me a psycho slut killer. Regardless of how others perceived me, I had to figure out how I saw myself. I struggle to accept my victimhood.

Many ladies in prison with me were guilty of their crimes. Some were overcharged and overpunished, but I believed one of my cellmates when she said she didn't realize her luggage set's lining, a gift from her new partner, hid cocaine. Most offenders confessed. Professional thieves, prostitutes, and drug traffickers were proud of their crimes. One of my cellmates, a pickpocket a few years older than me, gleefully remembered stealing three mopeds in one day to go about the city. Another Roma woman told me she had seen me walking around Perugia in the weeks before I was detained and considered taking my backpack, but decided I wasn't carrying anything valuable. (She was right)

Women left a trail of victims. They were imprisoned for that. I learned that many of them were victims before they committed crimes as I got to know them. They were poor, neglected, abused. They learned to exploit after being abused. After being harmed, they stopped caring how they hurt others. They were cynical and combative due to entitlement and defeat. The World vs. Me.

When I got home from prison, "victimhood" was a cultural issue. While the powerful were calling allegations witch hunts, I observed people wearing various degrees of unfairness and disadvantage like scout merit badges. These victimhood theories didn't fit my reality.

I suffered wrongful imprisonment and significant reputational damage. My youth and innocence were taken, changing my life. Even when I contemplated how terribly I'd been fucked over and witnessed my friends incorporating their disadvantages into their identities, the world told me I wasn't a victim. The real victim was Meredith.

My time with the ladies in Capanne jail, the parallel to Meredith's victimhood, the possibility that Meredith and I could have exchanged places, and being forced to shut up and disappear shape my view of my victimization. My childhood joys and chances have made me grateful. It's made me appreciate life. It's taught me that injustice made me stronger and that hatred (which continues) couldn't break me. Only made me stronger.

Victimhood can be viewed without zero-sum comparison. Kintsugi was introduced to me when I studied Japanese as a teenager. Gold metalwork reinforces and emphasizes fissures in shattered bowls and vases. These bowls are stronger and prettier. Today I see my victimhood this way. Most importantly, kintsugi bowls don't fix themselves. They demand care, talent, and artistic refinement. Agency helps here.

Being a victim never satisfied me because it didn't say anything about my character or activities. It didn't describe me. It was just my experience. My work to fuse my fissures with gold shows who I am and what I cherish. I'm not resentful or humiliated about my traumas. I couldn't fathom life without them. My greatest strength comes from them, so I wouldn't remove them.

The Stoic philosopher Seneca famously observed, "I judge you unfortunate because you have never lived through misfortune." You have lived without an opponent—no one, not even you, knows your potential." He realized tough times shape us. Survivors of trial by fire can have a deeper insight of themselves.

We should still feel sorry when we experience tragedy and adversity. It implies that we shouldn't feel exclusively bad emotions. I like that victimhood embrace. I can carry Meredith's unpleasant legacy more readily.

I want it otherwise, but her identity has become so intertwined with mine that most people can't think of me without thinking of her, or vice versa. I never wanted this burden, and it's awkward because I didn't know Meredith well. But I feel privileged that I got to know her briefly for who she was, rather than only in the context of her murder, like millions who know her name. Meredith is crucial to my trauma, but she did not cause it. I remember her as part of the gold filigree that holds my broken parts together.

CHAPTER 35
The Art of Freedom

A few friends invited us to supper weeks after I returned from Italy, ready to hear everything. Eureka crawled while we sat on the couch. Chris and I told them what happened, and then the critical question: "How do you feel?"

I said I felt very light. I crossed a 2007 subconscious box. The tale required this ending. After a decade of surviving and attempting to not do what I was accused of, I felt like I had done something. It was fantastic to create something new and unnecessary.

Afterward, I'd be lying if I didn't want what I didn't get. My apologies was not received. No one admitted guilt. I didn't hear him publicly declare my innocence. However, I've learnt that good things take time while negative things happen instantly. Change takes time. Growth requires time. I gave Giuliano a significant transformation opportunity he wasn't ready for. I gave him a challenge he never imagined.

I keep reminding myself that it's not about what I or he deserves because I turn my head and think that way. I remind myself that blaming and punishment rarely resolve disagreement or help people learn from their mistakes. Giuliano thought he could damage me because of his thinking. He thought I deserved years of pain because someone had to be punished. If the punishment for such a crime was rehabilitation and release when no longer a threat to society, I would have been released the day I was caught.

Our letters have continued, and I often use the open-ended encouragement I acquired as a parent: compassionately observing, softly guiding, sprinkling recommendations and nuggets of knowledge. For instance, true apologies are specific and without excuse; everything you say before "but" doesn't count; we are what we do and how we act; it's tragically easy to cause great harm while thinking we're doing the right thing; and when we feel righteous, we must be humble and self-aware

Giuliano sometimes grumbles and rolls his eyes like a teen in his letters. I listen to him make excuses, blame others, dodge clear questions, and say I don't understand Italian law. I see him craving for my acceptance, comfort, and affection. I keep giving it to him.

Trying to accept the apology I won't get. Closure and how my profound scars will affect my life are on my mind. I wish to avoid revisiting my pain. I still cry when I speak for the Innocence Project or share my podcast with someone who knows how it feels to be completely lost. For better or worse, I know my unpleasant experience has value, and I've been lucky enough to make meaning of it and offer others insight.

For years, I thought obtaining closure over Italy meant letting go of my trauma. This is my strength, I now realize. Psychologically and physically, humans are resilient. Our bones repair themselves stronger after breaking. Our psyches heal with serenity, perspective, and power after breaking. Just as I wouldn't like you to break your bones to strengthen them, I wouldn't wish my false conviction on anyone. I wouldn't change it for anything. I know we don't choose our traumas either. Our losses are varied, but we all lose loved ones, innocence, and who we used to be.

It's a losing game to avoid losing anything or everything. You will eventually. The only way to win is to accept loss as the negative space that helps us appreciate life's joys, loves, and people. My son Echo was born in September 2023, making me a mother of two. I see my youthful energy in him and Eureka, both of whom are warm and caring toward a world that has been kind to them, even if I know someone will be terrible to them. They'll suffer. I can't stop it. I hope their trauma is less severe than mine. I hope their hardships make them stronger and nicer. I hope that frees them.

Freedom is a practice, I've learned. I practice freedom by accepting the grace of a God I don't believe in, which none of us deserve. Catholics say that. I believe we deserve grace, kindness, and forgiveness regardless of who we are, what we've done, or what we haven't done.

Kindness is hard, especially to people who have wronged us. It's liberating. In my most Zen moments, my gaze dissolves suffering. It reappears eventually. I must be kind to myself then. Life is hard! Caring for your own mistakes is harder than for those who harm you. I remind myself that kindness demands guts, not fearlessness, but acting despite it. As I do this, I wonder if I'm making progress. To end suffering, find closure, and heal trauma, I have no answers. I don't know true freedom.

I can try. Your hardship increases your chance to be free, I know. I found purpose, a humbling and uplifting viewpoint, and the ability to forgive myself and others after my darkest experience. I found a way out of arrogance, resentment, and hatred—all sources of pointless misery.

Long ago, I felt trapped in a life I didn't create. I desperately tried not to be Foxy Knoxy, the insane slut killer, and then similarly not to be "the girl accused of murder." I'm free from an unwanted life. I don't define myself by my failures. Instead, I define my life daily.

Just what does that mean? Most of us believe that freedom involves making individual choices without external constraint. Even without the philosophical issue of free choice, being coercion-free is significant, but it doesn't convey what matters most to me. This is my preferred view:

To be free is to be aware of how we are immersed in our circumstances.

A Benediction

May you never confuse kindness with weakness.

May you accept the apology you will never get.

May you choose to give when you don't yet know what you want or need.

May you reach for the stars so that in failure you walk on the moon.

May you choose, at the fork in the road, the path that will change you.

May you expect others to be worthy of respect,

even as they act without honor,

and may those around you expect your best

even when you are at your worst,

for expectation is a doorway.

May your courage be compassionate.

May your compassion be curious.

May your curiosity be courageous.

May your enemies become friends,

or if not friends, then fools,

for we are all fools at times,

and may you find wisdom in the fool's mouth.

May you choose the company of those you want to succeed,

and who will roll in the mud with you when you fall.

May you yes, and your life.

May your pain clear the fog that has you walking in circles.

May you remember that you are not alone even when you are alone.

May you forgive yourself.

May you be free from suffering.

May you be free to grow, change, love.

May you be free.

May you be free.

May you be free.

Printed in Dunstable, United Kingdom